SHARE A SMILE

Thriving in Life and Treatment

ELICIA RAPRAGER

SHARE A SMILE

Copyright © 2020 Elicia Raprager

All rights reserved.

ISBN: 978-0-578-78120-4

Library of Congress Control Number: 2020919866

Design by Transcendent Publishing

Editing by Dana Micheli

Author Photo by Jordan Alexandria
Studio: The Yellow Bucket

DISCLAIMER: *Although this book has been reviewed for accuracy by a mental health professional, it is not intended as a substitute for the medical advice of a medical professional. The reader is advised to regularly consult a physician in matters relating to his/her health and particularly with respect to any symptoms that may require medical attention.*

Printed in the United States of America.

DEDICATION

This book is dedicated to those who have been misunderstood and need to be heard. You are an extraordinary work-in-progress. It is also dedicated to those on the outside looking in. You are essential and appreciated. Finally, this book is dedicated to family members who have passed, but who greatly influenced me and the woman I have become.

ACKNOWLEDGMENTS

Thanks to Mom and Mark; Dad and Teresa; Kallene and Brian; Justin and Shinda; Chris; Jessica; Sandra; Ash; Mandee; Joe Harmon, MA, LPC; Dr. Hannon; Dr. Hutton; Dr. Burkland; Dr. Kresch; Dr. Steinman; Shanda Trofe; Dana Micheli; Kyra and Todd Schaefer; Chelly; Marilynn; Ghenet; Pam; Raina; and my language arts teachers. I also thank the rest of my family and friends – you know who you are.

Special thanks to everyone who gave a little or a lot
to help me publish this book.

You made my dream a reality.

CONTENTS

INTRODUCTION

Who I Was and Who I've Become

I'm desperately in need of sleep, but my mind has too many cruel things to say. My eyes are dry and sore. I haven't gotten out of bed to use the bathroom or feed Nala, my cat. It was suggested that I take time off and that's what I'm doing, though I'm painfully aware that my to-do list is growing by the minute. My pajama shirt and pillowcase are soggy from endless sobbing. The sheets smell a little stale, but I can't bring myself to wash a load of laundry. I'm glad my husband and friends are at work, because my mood brings others down. Only Nala remains my constant companion.

My phone screen lights up. *How are you?*

I consider replying to my dad's text. I could tell him I've been wearing the same pajamas for days. I could send him a picture of used tissues and empty wrappers covering my side of the bedroom, and tell him I've been subsisting on fruit snacks and chocolate. My stomach can't handle much, and besides, microwaving a meal seems like too much work. I could tell my dad that I miss him and I don't know how much longer I can go on feeling this way, but I don't want him to worry.

Okay. Just resting. Love you.

I was supposed to be using my time off to get out in nature. I was supposed to find my passion and confidence, but I simply wasn't feeling well enough, at least not those first few days.

I wasn't really unworthy. I didn't actually bring others down. I was just being bullied by my insecurities. Does this sound familiar?

You are an amazing individual. Depression and anxiety might hide that truth from you. I couldn't see it back then. There were days when my bed was my only sanctuary, days when I laid there so long I didn't know if it was night or morning.

After I stopped denying my conditions, I started going to therapy. I started learning from others. There are still challenging moments and days, but now I am able to cope. I started to become more confident, stronger and happier.

I faced my fears. On the night of my birthday, I went to an outdoor concert with my husband and two friends. It was hours from our home, something I would usually be apprehensive about. Before the concert, we went to a Mexican restaurant. The waiter brought out a beautiful, delicious dessert to celebrate the occasion. There is a picture of me smiling, about to dip my spoon into the mountain of ice cream drizzled with chocolate syrup. It was the most genuine smile I'd made in several months. I wasn't concerned about my crooked teeth or an unlikely act of terror. *I was happy.* To me, that moment was about excitement, friendship, indulgence and freedom. Today, happiness has become my new normal, and my gratitude is so deep and profound it is hard to put into words.

I didn't get to this point overnight; it was a long, hard-won battle that began with a question asked by my counselor: "If you didn't have Major Depressive Disorder (MDD) or other things burdening you, how would you be different?"

I told him I'd be less tired. I'd do more things that I enjoy. I'd feel better about myself and visit with family and friends more, without needing to lay down or go into a quiet room.

You probably don't want to be reclusive any more than I did.

You want to be free of that feeling of guilt, shame, sorrow, fear and doubt all woven together into a heavy blanket. This blanket traps and suffocates, but it also soothes and calms as well. The longer it covers you, the heavier and warmer it becomes, like an extra comforter that keeps you in bed longer on a cold day. It becomes a piece of you.

In the pages that follow, I share my journey with anxiety and depression, as well as a variety of tools that helped me lift that blanket from my shoulders. Throughout my teen years, my mom repeatedly told me, "For God's sake, Elicia! Grow a damn backbone." I had a backbone; what I needed was an exoskeleton to protect me from the outside elements. In my mid-to-late twenties, I was equipped with a metaphorical, protective layer. That, I will also share with you.

Once I started feeling better and more like myself, I realized I had wasted years of time! This realization was my "aha moment." This was not just a reset, but a complete reimagining of my life. I started gaining more knowledge, and appreciation, for my experiences. I started setting goals again, for my hobbies, work and homelife. It felt amazing – a milestone in and of itself! I wanted to become the best version of myself.

I also began to shed the feelings of guilt that many people with mental illness have. It is the worry that the baggage you carry around, you also place on the shoulders of your loved ones. Thinking about the disappointment and sorrow I caused them used to paralyze me and keep me from going to parties and work functions. Now, I'm managing those symptoms. I'm enjoying the precious time I have with my family and friends.

It is my hope that this book will also help you reclaim your life from the clutches of depression and anxiety. I encourage you to respond to the writing prompts, and in reading about my experiences take comfort in the fact that you are not alone. You owe it to yourself to start living again, and I hope that reading this book will be a part of that new beginning, just as writing it has been a huge part of mine. This book is also for the family and friends who witness these struggles, so that they too might understand and grow closer to their loved one battling mental health challenges.

I wish you all the best.

Sincerely,

Elicia

PART ONE

Denial

This is a difficult phase and one in which care is often refused. When you deny that your mental health is preventing you from living your daily life, you don't take the necessary actions to manage it. Your health can actually become worse during this phase.

Yet, there is hope. Family members and friends may be able to recognize the signs and encourage you to seek treatment. It's not easy to admit you're in denial. That requires a deep, sincere look at yourself. Ultimately, you'll only do this when you are ready. You might have to take that deep look a few times to convince yourself that something is not right.

Why? Because depression and anxiety *lie* to you.

Depression tells you that what you're feeling doesn't matter.

Anxiety tells you that you could be judged or feel worse by going to counseling or taking medication. When both are talking, you may feel exhausted and unwilling to take those steps. If you're stubborn like me, it is especially difficult to pry yourself from denial's firm grip.

Here are some behaviors to look for in yourself and others:
- Being overly defensive.
- Being apathetic.
- Being overly emotional.
- Being irrational and refusing to listen to or accept any logical argument about your behavior.

Here are some actions to help move away from denial and toward acceptance:
- Be honest with yourself.
- Write down any judgments you have and let those go. Judgment of yourself and others can deter you from accepting your mental health status at face value.
- Speak with someone you trust about reported concerns.
- Consider recent behaviors that don't match your usual lifestyle or morale.
- Be patient with yourself. Everyone goes at their own pace.

In the next three chapters, you will read about the events that led to the mismanagement of my depression and anxiety disorders. As with any medical condition, you'll see the importance of early diagnosis and treatment. Near the end of Part One, I will progress to Acceptance.

> "When denial is in play, a person simply refuses to recognize the truth, no matter how apparent."
> ~ Taite Adams[1]

---

[1] Adams, Taite. *E-Go: Ego Distancing Through Mindfulness, Emotional Intelligence, and the Language of Love.* (Rapid Response Press, 2014).

1

Bullied, but Stronger

In this chapter, you'll see how my childhood troubles weakened the foundation of my mental health. I tolerated years of "harmless" but cruel banter that stretched into young adulthood. I didn't want to fight with others; I didn't want to be the reason anyone felt insignificant or unworthy. I wanted to be the person whose compliment stays with someone long after it's said. I wanted my gestures to be paid forward. Eventually, I learned to stick up for myself and others.

A volleyball flew past me.

"Move!" I heard someone shout, "Hit the ball!"

Another girl complained, "God. She's just like a personal cone. Except even *that* has a purpose."

As my counselor would later tell me, feeling you have no purpose is depression doing its job.

I dreaded gym class. I was like that character in every high school movie trope – horrible at team sports and always the last one picked. My bony build gave credence to those claims. For years, I replaced the words "scrawny" with "svelte" and "skinny" with "athletic" – an early attempt to shift my thinking to the positive.

Bus rides weren't easy either. It was during one such ride when a fourth-grade girl announced that I had an extra toe on my left foot. Unfortunately, that rumor was true; even worse was that the girl was one of my friends. She held me down while a boy pulled off my shoe and sock to see for himself. The bus driver continued the route without saying a thing.

The rest of the day was not easy. With the quick wit all cruel children seem to have, someone decided my initials, E.T., now stood for "Extra Toe." The name stuck with me through junior high. Fast forward to junior high gym class, when another classmate said he'd like to cut off my toe and sell it on eBay. What is wrong with people? The health teacher added fuel to the fire. She told us such birth defects were caused by parents smoking crack. Of course, my parents didn't. I tearfully told them what happened, and my health teacher received hell the same afternoon. I'm fortunate to have supportive parents.

My big brother, Justin, poked fun at me too, telling me that I was from "Planet Six Toe" and our parents had adopted me. He also said that if I was bad they would ship me back. He meant no harm, but I was so inconsolable my parents had to break out my birth certificate to prove I was *their* child, born in Flint, Michigan, not on some made-up planet. I must have looked adorably ridiculous. I was only seven years old.

When I complained about my foot anomaly, my paternal grandparents informed me that I could have had the extra toe removed as an infant. Since my toe has a bone in it, it would have required a surgical procedure. The hospital told my parents they would have to sign a waiver, absolving the hospital from liability if I didn't wake up after the procedure. They refused.

As a child, I wished I didn't have to go through the harassment and feel like a freak. As an adult, I'm grateful to have wonderful parents who protected me. If I'd had that procedure and something went wrong, I would have missed so many things, so many good times with my family and friends. I wouldn't be sharing my message with you.

My family tried to make me feel better. My paternal grandpa told me Marilyn Monroe was born with an extra toe and had it removed as a teenager. I was comforted by that; clearly the toe had not stopped her from being famous and beautiful. Later, I learned it was just a rumor.

I remember accompanying my mom to the Shiawassee Art Gallery. One particular painting caught my eye. It was a barefoot angel standing next to a wolf or leopard, I don't remember which. Like me, the angel had long blonde hair and blue eyes, but the most stunning detail was an extra toe! I was awestruck. From an early age, my paternal aunt and maternal grandma had encouraged my adoration of angels and cherubs, and to me this felt like some sort of positive sign. Angels helped me feel safe.

Ernest Hemingway had a home for six-toed cats. This too helped me feel a little better. After all, those cats must be special to have an entire building dedicated to them.

Then there were the experiences that continued to make me feel as though I was from Planet Six Toe. For example, the time I was barefoot in my boyfriend's fraternity and one of his fraternity brothers looked at my foot and froze. He apologized, but said he couldn't be in the same room while I was barefoot. I was completely shocked. By then I was used to odd looks and questions from children, but a college guy, afraid of a toe?

When I was little, I fractured my sixth toe while riding a jet ski with my dad, brother and friend. When the doctor examined my toe, she didn't understand how it was hanging so far to the left. My dad and I told the doctor to count. She did so, then started to smile. My dad and I told her to count again. She recounted and her smile broke through both cheeks. The doctor excused herself and closed the door. Laughter boomed on the other side. All those years in medical school and she was stumped by my special feature! Although the break was painful, I was glad to be excused from gym class.

Now that I'm in my late twenties, my toe only bothers me for logical reasons, like when I shop for shoes. Few shoes feel comfortable on my left foot. I'm considering having it removed for that reason. On the other hand, I'm nervous about going under the knife and don't see it happening soon.

Extra toe aside, I wasn't too fond of the rest of my body. I was always underweight. My dad passed me off as younger throughout high school to get the kids' price for tickets to local events. I wasn't happy about being fourteen and passing for ten or eleven. I was in high school and wanted to be attractive to boys my age.

Even worse was that my weight earned me unwanted attention from classmates, who accused me of being both anorexic and bulimic. The truth was, I was a picky eater and had a fast metabolism (even as an adult, my wrists are barely two inches wide. I'm not upset about it, but it would be nice to wear a bracelet that doesn't slide down to my elbow when I fix my hair or reach for something above my head), but it didn't matter. When a couple of years later we watched videos on eating disorders, I was relieved that the class was taught by a different health teacher.

Freshman year of high school, I had the biggest crush on this boy. I was the new, quiet, nerdy girl. He was funny, cute, and nerdy too, but in a cool way. I fit in with his friends. Everyone knew I liked him, so I was crushed when a girl said to me, "You're flat-chested. You don't have a chance with him. Maybe, if you straighten your teeth and get breast implants, he'd like you."

Though I don't remember the name of that girl, I can still hear her words ringing in my ears.

If we'd had the money, I probably would have asked my mom to let me do those things. Now I'm grateful I didn't. I am married to Chris, who loves me and has been with me through everything I share in this book. He loves me for me, just as I am. That helps me like who I am too.

Back then, I was timid and I let others define my worth. Now, I would gladly stand up for myself and tell them; *It's my toe. I'm small-framed and I've done nothing to hurt you. I don't want to hear you say anything like that again.*

Once I started standing up for myself and articulating why I didn't deserve cruelty, my self-esteem scaled the walls.

In college, I took an advertising class. I loved it. I had creative freedom. Everyone needed to write and record a thirty-second Public Service Announcement. It only took me a few seconds to think of my topic: bullying awareness and suicide prevention. My mom recorded it on my first smartphone. You can see me give my mom a less-than-subtle cue to stop recording. To watch it from the correct angle, you need to tilt your head. Still, I'm proud of it.

I held pieces of paper, each with a significant milestone: Graduation; Job Promotion; Your Wedding Day; and New Baby. Then I let go of the papers and let them flutter to the floor.

"Every day, there is a child who stays home from school to avoid his or her bully. This happens in the workplace too. Too often these victims take their own lives to escape it all. To the bullied, there are great milestones ahead." I lifted the strips of paper and said, "To the bullied: Don't take these away. Please. Call your local hotline if you're in need."

I thought about showing my video on the monitors on campus. My professor supported me, but let me know that the school had to approve such content and I would need to go through hoops to get my PSA video on there. I didn't try it, a decision I would come to regret.

I thought about going to elementary and middle schools to

share my story and empower the children who needed it. But unlike other kids and teenagers, I had never been physically hurt and decided that this made my experiences and words less valuable. Really, though, I was just underestimating my own worth, which of course was due in part to the bullying I'd endured.

These bullies weren't monsters. They were kids, with their own insecurities and wounds. Nevertheless, the impressions they made lasted and became the framing of my mental instability. They're the reason I over-analyze what I say, wear closed-toe shoes, and apologize for simply being myself. Another part of anxiety is apologizing for no reason. You overthink and worry about everything you say and do. When something isn't right, you say sorry, even if there's no need. Is that something you do? If so, I understand.

Oddly enough, I am grateful to my bullies. Those memories remind me to be kind to everyone I meet. I want to be able to say something good about everyone. I said it earlier and I'll say it again: You're amazing. I hope soon enough, you realize it.

The Reality of Imposter Syndrome

Why do successful people often feel that they haven't earned their position or that their accomplishments are disingenuous? Imposter Syndrome is to blame. This is not a disorder, but more of a reaction or belief.

The first time I learned about it was from a close friend, Sandra. When she told me she had Imposter Syndrome and explained what it was, I could hardly believe it. She is talented, intelligent, beautiful, and free-thinking. How could she feel like a fake and unworthy of her accomplishments? As I spoke with her, I recognized that I too felt like an imposter at times. I didn't feel worthy to speak to a high school class. I was terrified to show anyone my first draft of this book. I didn't feel right calling myself a bestselling author, even though I am.

I am a contributing author to the compilation book, *Inspirations: 101 Uplifting Stories for Daily Happiness*, published in 2019. When it reached bestseller status, the publisher couldn't wait to tell everyone that we were now "bestselling authors." Though I was overjoyed, I couldn't help but feel as though I hadn't earned that title. I also realized the syndrome was in play when I decided to end my college education early.

Since then, Sandra and I make it a point to remind each other that we're genuine and worthy of our successes. They weren't by luck or by coincidence. We earned them. We're talented and proud of it. Imposter syndrome can take a hike.

If you find this imposter intruding on your victories, I hope you remember that you worked for those victories. You are deserving. Appreciate yourself and be grateful you're you.

As my Grandma T. says, "You do wonders, honey." Always remember the kind words from those who matter most.

Review and Reflect

Please take some time to think about an unpleasant experience, whether it happened last week, last year, or when you were a child. What did you learn from it and how have you applied that lesson to your life? If you haven't applied it, write a brief plan to do so. You've got this.

_____

_____

_____

2

Night Terrors and Sleep Paralysis

In this chapter, you'll see how years of sleep disturbances affected my physical and mental health. I researched sleep disorders to see how I could improve my quality of sleep and, like any condition, a couple of the "solutions" made matters worse. Eventually I did find what works for me, and these days I sleep fairly well, often going about two months without trouble.

I used to sit in the dark, not realizing how much time went by. This worried my husband Chris, and he would come out, turn on the light, and try to get me to watch TV, color or just watch him play a game. Chris and his friends are gamers. When he was away at game nights and gaming conventions, I used to lean on my friends. I would go to Jessica's house or go out to eat with Sandra. If it was a whole weekend or longer, I would go to my mom's. I needed company. I needed comfort. I needed entertainment.

I would go without food, I would go without water, and I didn't care. The fact that I didn't care made me nervous, so in time I learned to become more mindful. If I started to feel stuck, apathetic, or lonely, I would call my mom or grandparents, or pour myself a glass of water. Sometimes I just got up and wandered the house so I wasn't sitting in one place. If I noticed this around nightfall, I would turn on the light so I wouldn't be in the dark.

Now that I know what to look for and have learned more about my likes and interests, I can entertain and self-soothe. When Chris is away, I'll write, watch a favorite movie, draw, or play with Nala; sometimes, I even look forward to having time to myself. It's quiet and I get a lot done. I get a feeling of accomplishment. One time, I posted a video of my dining room and kitchen after I cleaned it. This was a huge win for me, because I used to just wait for the day to pass. That day I was determined to be productive. I put on music, lit a candle, and sang to rock songs while I washed the dishes and swept the floor. I even wiped the table and scrubbed the refrigerator. It was something insignificant to most, but it was a big leap toward progress and independence for me.

I used to keep all the window blinds closed during the day. Everyone told me sunshine would lift my mood, but I was afraid that someone would look in the house. For years, I considered myself a victim, and then it happened: I was a victim of a lawsuit, a victim of a car break-in, and a victim of my own hatred.

I grew up in what most believed to be a haunted house. I knew it to be true, and felt whatever it was wanted to scare and hurt me. After my parents divorced in 2001, my mom got full custody of me. When it was time to stay the weekend with my dad, I would become ill before leaving home or soon after arriving at his place. I would throw up, have diarrhea, stomach pains, and migraines. I was afraid of the house and what was inside.

Oftentimes, my dad would have to come home early from business meetings because I called him hysterically crying. My friends and I would run out of the house screaming, and for years I even thought "it" followed me and haunted me in my dreams. I thought only something evil could be the reason behind this terror.

Though I was nervous about talking about it, I eventually gave my psychiatrist a glimpse of this reality. After all, I was there to be honest and get help. She wrote "psychosis" on my intake form.

Thank goodness I hadn't told her about the first night it happened.

I was eight or nine years old. Rain was pounding on my window and the growl of thunder was growing closer and closer.

Suddenly, I saw a terrifying form standing in the hallway outside my room.

"Don't come out!" I yelled, afraid for my parents. "He's got a knife!"

He was a pale man with long hair, wearing a black and white striped prison uniform. His fingers were curled around a large knife. After I called out he peeked into my room. My heart jumped out of my chest and my eyes stayed fixated on this stranger. My terror increased when I heard my parents' door rattle and open. Would the man hurt them? Suddenly, the hallway was flooded with light and my dad was standing there, looking at me with concern. The creepy man was gone.

The next morning, I overheard my mom telling my dad and brother about her experiences in the house. She had seen the same presence! After the divorce, every girlfriend my dad brought to the house felt, heard, or saw something. My dad did too. One day, I was in my room playing with my dollhouse, which was about two feet away from the door. Suddenly, I felt a sting on my left wrist. It was bleeding, just a smidge. Even after my family started acknowledging what was happening, they insisted it couldn't physically hurt us. I still have a faint two-inch scar that makes me think otherwise.

When she heard about my experiences, my aunt on my dad's side bought me a crystal angel with a dangling gold bell. It came with a calming message.

"Each time a bell rings, an angel gains its wings."

I placed the angel on the post of my canopy bed and rang the bell when I felt scared, which provided some relief. A few days later, the bell went missing. I looked all around my room for it. I never found it. My older brother swore he didn't take the angel's bell. I thought a presence might have hidden it from me.

I continued to experience night terrors well into adulthood and, determined to find help, I read several articles on the topic. I learned that night terrors are quite common for adults with mental illnesses such as depression, panic disorder, and PTSD. Over the years, I've sleepwalked, screamed, talked, flailed, punched, cried and have had panic attacks in my sleep. I also learned sleep disorders can be hereditary, which resonated because my mom has had sleep disturbances as well. One night, while sound asleep, my sweet mother held a kitchen knife as she walked to the side door and opened it to no one. My dad woke up and, understandably startled, took the knife from Mom and walked her back to bed.

My strange nighttime experiences continued long after I stopped spending weekends at that house. Once, for about a week, I woke myself and my husband by repeatedly saying, "Help me," in a voice that didn't sound like my own. This disturbed both of us. Over the years, Chris has helped me through countless panic attacks. In fact, it was happening so frequently that I trained myself to say, "Wake me up!" Often, this came out as a panicked scream. He would comfort me and tell me he was with me; sometimes, he just rested his upper body against mine, which stopped me from kicking and thrashing. Sometimes, I woke up; other times, I continued calmly sleeping. Sometimes, I just felt for him.

There have been times when I've had nightmares for five consecutive days, and on and off for two weeks. According to *The New York Times*, only one in five hundred adults has even one nightmare a week.[2] I guess this is something else that makes me

---

[2] Goleman, Dan. "Nightmares are Linked to Creativity in New View." New York Times, October 23, 1984, sec. C. https://www.nytimes.com/1984/10/23/science/nightmares-are-linked-to-creativity-

special. My Grandpa T told me he used to dream that a wolf was chasing him. In one dream, the wolf caught him, and after that he never had the dream again.

I tried different methods to improve my sleep. A couple of years ago, an acquaintance gave me liquid melatonin. I did some research on its possible side effects and learned that some people had bizarre dreams while taking it and others reported it helped them to sleep well. Since I already had frequent nightmares, I didn't see any harm in taking the melatonin. I added two drops to my tea before bed, hoping I would feel at ease and naturally drift off into a dreamless sleep. Instead, I stayed awake for the entire night. Yet, for some reason, I didn't feel tired the next day.

I also talked with my family doctor and my counselor numerous times about what I referred to as my "chronic nightmares." They didn't find any correlation with stress, diet, duration of sleep, content watched before bed, or whether or not I was in a depressive state. In the meantime, I was afraid to fall asleep. I didn't want to find myself in a horrible dream again, where I felt and witnessed excruciating pain. In fact, sometimes after a week or two of terrifying dreams, I wouldn't sleep the next two nights. From experience, I know that lack of sleep triggers my Generalized Anxiety Disorder (GAD) and deepens my Major Depressive Disorder (MDD). I was desperate to find a solution.

When I told my psychiatrist about my eventful nights, she diagnosed me with "PTSD nightmares" and prescribed me something for it. It was the same medication one of my work friends had taken for several months and found quite helpful. I learned that the medication is primarily used to lower blood pressure. Unfortunately, I'd had issues with low blood pressure in the past and sure

---

in-new-view.html.

enough, after a week of taking the medication I started getting mild to moderate headaches. I was dizzy in the morning and nauseous throughout the day. The longer I took the medication, the worse the side effects became. When I told my psychiatrist about my side effects and medical history, she discontinued the medication. She also told me all medications that relieve nightmares reduce blood pressure. I had no choice but to deal with the frightening dreams.

My counselor asked me if I thought a sleep study would be helpful. Sleep apnea is prevalent in my family; I know this because a few of my immediate family members have had sleep studies done for that reason. Though I understand that a sleep study might benefit me, I am uncomfortable with the idea. I can't imagine getting any sleep in a hospital room, hooked up to various machines and separated from my husband. My dad told me about his experience, how loud the machines were and how frequently he woke up. My doctor said it's possible to do one at home, and one day I may consider that. In the meantime, I decided to do what I could to sleep better.

Here is a list of actions I've taken to improve the quality of my sleep:

- Took natural supplements
- Took prescription medication
- Practiced sleep meditations
- Received massages from my spouse
- Reset my circadian rhythm by going to bed and waking up earlier
- Visualized sending the people and creatures of my dreams away
- Wrote down my concerns and hopes before bed
- Watched cute animal videos before bed

- Exercised once a week or more
- Practiced beginner's yoga before bed
- Sipped "Sleepy Time tea" before bed
- Hung dreamcatchers
- Quit watching horror movies in 2012
- Quit reading horror and suspense books in 2012
- Stopped watching most of the news in 2015
- Used dream analysis to try to understand my nightmares
- Attempted lucid dreaming so I could give myself permission to wake up
- Prayed while holding a prayer rosary (a college friend gave me the bracelet)

Since I am an artist and a writer, I was curious to see if my creativity makes me more susceptible to sleep disorders. According to the same New York Times article, it does.[3] The author also connects creativity to schizophrenia; however, I am not suggesting this is the case.

As disturbing as they were, none of my previous sleep issues could have prepared me for my experience with sleep paralysis. It first happened one morning about six years ago, after Chris had left for work. I was still in bed, as I didn't have to leave for a few hours. The bedroom door was open just enough for Nala to enter and exit as she pleased. The gap slowly grew, but our fluffy cat wasn't the reason. I tried to sit up, but couldn't. My arms were locked.

A small, grotesque woman with slouched posture and tattered clothing walked through the door. My car keys and pepper spray were four inches from my head, but I was frozen, unable to reach for them.

---

[3] *Ibid.*

The woman continued to creep into our bedroom. She carried a wooden cutting board down by her knees. She stood at my side of the bed, mere inches from my face. I was so petrified I felt as though I had stopped breathing.

The woman, I saw, had been hurt. Her face was bruised in various colors. She had scabs and gashes on her cheek and jaw. Plus, one eye appeared to be swollen closed. At that moment, I was no longer fearful of how this woman got into our apartment. I wondered what had happened to her. After what seemed like several minutes, I was able to tilt my head away and I regained control of my hands. The woman left.

Unbelievably, I fell back asleep and was seemingly transported back in time. I saw the door open again and the same woman started to enter. I used all my strength to move my arms and turn my neck. The woman left once more.

A subsequent Google search revealed that many people believe this type of incident is demonic. I looked for a more logical explanation and learned that sleep paralysis happens when the body transitions from dream mode to being awake.[4] Instead of summarizing the scientific explanation, I suggest you read it for yourself.

When I looked for ways to prevent sleep paralysis, I was shocked to find instructions to help *trigger* it. Why would anyone want to feel these horrifying sensations? I didn't know, but I took those instructions and flipped them, doing the opposite. If these tools don't help you, they may at least give you ideas.

- Got out of bed when my husband left for work
- Avoided sleeping on my back

4 Pappas, Stephanie. "Brain Chemicals That Cause Sleep Paralysis Discovered." Live Science, July 17, 2012. https://www.livescience.com/21653-brain-chemicals-sleep-paralysis.html

- Avoided sleeping with my arms above my head
- Stopped sleeping with my hands beneath my pillow
- Stopped sleeping with my hands between my knees
- Stopped trying to physically fight the symptoms
- Told myself I'm awake and not in danger
- Made sure our television and stereo were turned off
- Closed the bedroom door and closet door

Thankfully, sleep paralysis hasn't been an issue for me since 2015. I have however, experienced auditory hallucinations when, stuck between REM sleep and waking up, I thought voices on the neighbor's TV were men talking in the apartment. Thankfully, this ended after we moved into our first rental house. More recently, I've experienced thrashing, talking and punching, a topic I've written about on my blog.

After being stuck in this hell loop, I was bound to have, and certainly deserving of, a good dream. In it, I was married to Jason Momoa. We were sitting with my mom and relatives from her side of the family. I leaned into his chest like I do with my real-life husband. As most would imagine, it was quite enjoyable!

If you would like to know more about night terrors, please visit the American Sleep Association website.[5] Their purpose is to bring awareness about sleep disorders.

---

[5] ASA Authors & Reviewers. "Night Terrors: Causes, Symptoms, & Treatments." https://www.sleepassociation.org/sleep-disorders-n/night-terrors/

Review and Reflect

Has there been a time in your life when fear got the best of you?

What physical fight or flight responses did you have?

_____

_____

_____

_____

_____

Was the fear imagined or real? Explain.

_____

_____

_____

_____

_____

How long did it take for you to feel safe again?

_____

_____

_____

_____

_____

3

The 100-Year Flood and a Possible Heart Attack

I can't believe you're doing this.

I can barely breathe. My heart is going a million miles per minute; my face and chest are tight and burning. I'm scared and in pain, yet as I'm admitted to the Detroit Medical Center Receiving, I am more concerned with the burly police officer intruding on my personal space and my privacy.

"Your purse!" he barks, his hand outstretched.

He quickly goes through the different pockets and removes the pepper spray my dad had bought for me.

"Am I going to get that back?" I meekly asked.

"No."

I bow my head and try to ignore the screams of a gunshot patient a few beds down. Beside me, my best friend Jessica reaches out her hand to clasp mine; with her other hand she pulls out her cell phone and calls Chris.

After examining me, a nurse hooks me up to an IV. He says I am dehydrated and need to rest. He explains that the IV fluids are replenishing my body. Finally, feeling calmer but unsure what has caused this incident, I drift off. When I wake, Chris is next to Jessica. He is holding my purse and looking at me with concern and relief. A doctor and a different nurse come in and tell me I had an anxiety attack that caused my heart to "flip out"; they then give me referrals to a cardiologist and a mental health clinic. At the time, I didn't know anyone who saw a counselor, and other than the one appointed by a Friend of the Court during my parents' divorce, I had never spoken to one either. Now, I adamantly refused to go. I didn't see the need for it or understand how counseling would help me.

That was in August of 2014. A month earlier, I had landed an office job that I loved (and still do). I was learning every day and had wonderful teammates and leaders. I was thrilled.

Then, a week before my hospital visit, I was caught in the "100-Year Flood." I left work at four o'clock and headed for Jessica's house in Metro-Detroit, as it was much closer than our apartment near Auburn Hills. Every road I tried to turn down was flooded or blocked by abandoned cars or a downed tree. I was lost, exhausted, hungry, and fearful that I wouldn't make it. It took me ten and a half hours to go ten miles.

At two-thirty in the morning I was only one intersection away from safety, food and rest, but the road was flooded. Jessica's fiancé suggested I leave my car and he would come to get me, but I didn't want to do that. I had seen countless abandoned cars and I couldn't do that to mine. They looked at different routes and found that was the only road I could take to get to them. The water was just above the tops of my tires. I heard it slosh and hoped with everything I had that I would make it safely to them. The seals kept the water out. I made it down the river of a road and turned on another main road. The water hadn't gotten to it.

"Relief!" I cried. "Guys. I'm going to make it. I can see your street."

I parked in front of their house and ran inside, where Jessica was waiting with a wonderful tuna fish pickle sandwich and juice. I had never in my life appreciated a meal so fully. Now I keep snacks in my car and purse for emergencies. It was my mom's idea.

I slept on their couch that night, and wore one of Jessica's dresses to work the next day. After work, we shopped for clothes and necessities as the area was still a mess and there was no way I was getting home. For the next four days, Jessica and I took back roads to get to and from work.

Moments before my ride in the ambulance, I was in the lunchroom, speaking with my insurance company and the auto shop about the flood damage to my car. I learned it would be at least a week before I got it back. This triggered my first panic attack. It wouldn't be my last.

I fell back into my chair and two nurses who were also on their lunch breaks came to my aid. My manager was informed of my attack. She asked me who else in the building she should contact, but I still couldn't speak.

One of the nurses spoke for me. "Contact Care Coordinator, Jessica."

Since the episode had seemed like a heart attack, I went to the cardiologist. I found out I had low blood pressure and needed to add sodium to my diet. He suggested that the next time I felt anxious to lay down and "eat a salt sandwich." He also recommended I drink Gatorade for the electrolytes and sodium. (Later, my neurologist would tell me the same to alleviate my migraines.) The cardiologist sent me to get an electrocardiogram, and that's when I learned that I have a benign heart murmur. The technician explained that my blood doesn't always circulate in and out of my heart as it should. Sometimes it stops and gurgles.

From there, I was referred to the most unpleasant test called the Tilt Table Test. They would strap me lying down to a table, then lift the table up into nearly a standing position before lowering me again. The objective was to get me to pass out; in fact, before the test I had to sign a consent form stating that if I didn't naturally pass out from the tilting movement, they could increase my heart rate to one hundred fifty-five beats per minute to get me to do so. Fun, right? No, it wasn't. I was extremely uncomfortable and felt sick, but didn't pass out. The technician informed me she was increasing my heart rate and I would lose consciousness.

When my test results came back abnormal, I was advised to wear an event monitor for thirty days. Trying to wear those with dresses and dress slacks was not easy or discreet. It would bounce off my chest as I walked. When I wore dress slacks, I clipped it to my belt buckle. I laughed at the number of times I hip-checked myself into doorways. Throughout the day or week, it would sing a little song while it sent my recordings to the doctor's office.

I found out that I have an irregular heart rate and my anxiety exacerbated it. More fun news. I also learned that I have vasovagal syncope. It's a type of dysautonomia that causes a person to become dizzy or faint. Thankfully, I learned my triggers and no longer experience symptoms.

Two months later, I had a similar episode at work. This time, I was struggling to find a Spanish-speaking specialist for a member. I felt pain and began to slide out of my chair. I messaged a team leader, who took over the call while I went to the restroom. Once there, I fell to the floor and couldn't get up easily. This time, I called my husband and he took me to the hospital. I'll never forget hearing one of the physicians say to another, "Twenty-four years old and complains of chest pain. I think she just wants to get out of work."

I didn't appreciate that remark. I am extremely uncomfortable in hospitals. I would have given anything to successfully finish the workday. Especially that day.

There was a woman in labor down the hall. She was having a rough, but quick delivery and her hollers made my husband and me cringe. Chris doesn't handle other people's blood or pain well – it gives him the heebie jeebies – but he always manages to make me laugh.

He looked at the needles in my arms and said, "Imagine they removed the needle and your veins came out with it."

It was so weird, I giggled in spite of the circumstances. I needed it.

When the doctor came in to explain my discharge paperwork, he asked if I'd contacted one of the mental health clinics that had been recommended during my last admission. I said I had not. He said I needed therapy, and his inflection suggested urgency.

Looking back, I didn't handle those situations well. Now, when I receive upsetting news, I write a plan. I've learned to control the way I react.

Today, if I received that phone call from my insurance company or mechanic, I would look at the situation at face value. I get my car in a week. I'm calm because I'm safe and staying with my best friend. We're going to carpool to work. That's part of the plan. I'm already feeling more in control. I don't have medication or clothes for the week, but I can communicate with my insurance and pharmacy to get an override. I'll buy some clothes after work. If that doesn't work, I could distract myself for the time being by reading or listening to music.

Another trick my counselor taught me is to hold something cold when I begin to panic. Maybe the reason it worked is because my body temperature would rise when I was anxious. Another reason could be that it drew my focus to the cold sensation spreading across my skin. I kept a small ice pack in the freezer at work, and when my trigger symptoms started, I'd grab that ice pack and hold it. It stopped them from escalating to a panic attack.

If I start to feel chest pain or an abnormally fast heart rate, I'll remind myself that it's common and I'm not going to die. I'll finish the task, take a break, hydrate myself, and focus on my breathing. You're probably thinking, *Not another book that talks about deep breaths and meditation.* It may sound cliché at this point, but the truth is that in certain situations it's beneficial. As we learned earlier, if I react poorly to my physical symptoms, my anxiety quickly becomes unmanageable. I don't want to feel that way again. I don't want you to go through it either.

Muting Myths About Post Traumatic Stress Disorder

As mentioned earlier, I was diagnosed with PTSD nightmares, as well as a twitch. I did not serve in the military, nor was I assaulted or abused – two generalizations made about people with this condition. Anyone at any age can witness or experience a trauma that leaves him or her with flashbacks, concerns it will happen again, and other symptoms. Trauma scars in more ways than one, so don't let someone deny you treatment because he or she is convinced that whatever happened isn't a real burden.

Review and Reflect

Think about a wound that isn't protected by a bandage. It's vulnerable to dirt and bacteria, and if not treated in time, it may become infected and result in more pain. Depression, anxiety, and other mental health conditions can also worsen if not taken seriously.

Have you or are you currently in denial about your mental state? If so, is it because you were worried about being stigmatized?

_____

_____

_____

_____

_____

_____

_____

Who or what group has or will support you during a transitional time?

_____

_____

_____

_____

_____

_____

What have you done or what can you do to move toward acceptance?

_____

_____

_____

_____

_____

_____

PART TWO

Acceptance

This is the phase where you recognize the significance of your mental health. You begin to take actions to strengthen it and protect it. Since you've graduated to acceptance, you'll slowly stop the concerning behaviors mentioned in Part One.

Family members and friends will start to see your improvements. They may tell you they're proud of you and encourage you to continue this process. They might also ask what they can do to help. Tell them, for their support is beneficial.

Here are some supportive ways family and friends can help you stay on track:

- Subscribe to a blog or email that sends educational information about mental health. My dad did this for me and it meant a lot to both of us.
- Know dates and times of appointments and promote accountability for attending appointments.
- If the provider allows it, be present as emotional support at the first appointment.
- Inquire about coping skills that were discussed during the appointment.
- Here are some things to remember when accepting your situation as it is:
- You are not a burden.

- You are worthy of a good life.
- You will still have difficult days. Learn from those days.
- There are several paths to wellness. Follow the path that you're comfortable taking.

In the next four chapters, you will read about my efforts to understand my mental health conditions and determine the appropriate treatments. You'll see that as in the case of many medical conditions, the first attempt may not always be ideal. Don't let this discourage you from trying other options. If you do, you won't find what works for you. Near the end of Part Two, I will progress to self-care and personal development.

"Acceptance doesn't mean resignation; it means understanding that something is what it is and that there's got to be a way through it."
~ Michael J. Fox[6]

---

[6] BrainyQuote, 2020. Retrieved January 30, 2020 from https://www.brainyquote.com/quotes/michael_j_fox_463873.

4

Three Referrals Later

After leaving the hospital, I saw my family doctor, showed her my discharge paperwork, and promptly broke down.

"I don't know what to do. I don't want to feel like this."

I told her I wanted to stay out of the hospital.

My doctor looked me in the eyes and said, "I think you have severe depression." She then recommended a few counselors.

My heart dropped. I couldn't believe this was happening to me.

With her words fresh in my mind, I contacted the recommended therapists and learned there was an opening at the clinic right down the road from our apartment. I decided I would go and try to get something out of it. I completed the new patient paperwork, then went into the counselor's room to find the stereotypical couch and a chair against the wall. The therapist's name was Joe. We greeted each other. Then I sat on the chair, wondering what I was going to talk about for fifty minutes. I was happily married. I had just gotten a great job. I had good relationships with my family. How could I *possibly* be depressed?

I tried to speak a few times, but wasn't ready. I think twenty minutes went by before I opened with being bullied in grade school, being a child of divorce, and the stress of starting my bachelor's degree. I talked about friendships that meant a lot to me. Friendships that had lasted for years and were now fading. We weren't talking much and I was afraid one childhood friend might be in an unhealthy relationship. I yearned to talk with her, but for several months my attempts at communication had been met with short texts like, *Can't talk right now. Miss you.*

In the therapist's office, I realized for the first time just how much her absence had been paining me. This girl was like my younger sister; we used to play hide and seek, bake awful desserts and make up our own songs. Her family was like my extended family and vice versa. It felt silly to say because she was alive and well, but it felt like she was gone, and I missed her.

Now blubbering, I looked up at Joe. He told me he'd helped many people.

"Have you helped people like me?"

"Oh, I've helped 'Elicias,'" he replied. He then said that though diagnosing was part of his job requirement, he didn't like doing it because he didn't want patients to overthink it. At the end of my first appointment, he wrote "Major Depressive Disorder (Mod. Recurring)" and "Panic Disorder" on a yellow Post-it note and handed it to me. I looked at the note, then back up at him.

"Why now? Why do I feel this way *now*?"

Joe explained that when our mind is at peace, it often decides to process thoughts it had locked away. This is why someone can be feeling great about life and also experience symptoms of depression.

In 2001, the World Health Organization published that one in four people have or will have a mental or neurological disorder. That year, four hundred-fifty million people were affected.[7]

---

[7] Sayers J. (2001). The world health report 2001 — Mental health: new understanding, new hope. *Bulletin of the World Health Organization*, *79*(11), 1085.

I told him that my mom was a "worry wart" and I am too.

"Panic disorder is more than just worrying," he said. "Anxiety is feeling unsafe. Depression is feeling you have no purpose."

I thought about my constant fear and loneliness during childhood. Those words resonated with me. Still, Joe would continue to remind me of this during several appointments.

He would also, every few appointments, ask me how I felt about seeing a psychiatrist. I knew a psychiatrist was likely to prescribe something and told him I preferred to be treated in other ways. I felt my depression and mood were situational – I had recently lost three cousins and a friend who lived in my neighborhood – and didn't want to take medications to cope.

I was also having trouble with my new school. I had graduated from a community college that was quite esteemed, and one of my business teachers recommended I transfer to an accredited university. When I went to the open house, I felt like I was at a used car dealership. A few of the older men poked their greedy fingers into my shoulder and told me, "I'm going to grow your wealth." I didn't want to be that type of businesswoman. I had dreams of inspiring others and opening a business to create and exhibit art and writing. Those advisors didn't match my giving and creative agenda.

Against my wise teacher's advice, I enrolled in a private school. The advisors and teachers I met were lovely. I thought it was the ideal school for me. I chose to enroll in the online school instead of travelling to Washtenaw or Ann Arbor. Unfortunately, the school wasn't as reputable as it had seemed. In the ten months I attended, I had three different academic advisors. Plus, the ombudsman took over one of the courses because the teacher had stopped showing. There were financial barriers as well. I dropped out, and though I knew on some level that it was the best decision at the time, it haunted me. Chris and my family supported my decision.

I stared at Joe's sticky note multiple times. I wondered how these two conditions that fit on such a small piece of paper could cause so much heartache and distress.

At a follow-up appointment with my family doctor, I showed her the note and suddenly found myself asking about a medication to ease the pain. She prescribed me a half dose of ten-milligram Citalopram, a commonly prescribed medication with very few known side effects. Seven months passed, seven months in which I only remember falling asleep and waking up. I was zombie-like, living in a blur of apathy. I didn't want to go out. Nothing sounded fun. Some nights, I nodded off as early as five-thirty or six p.m. I understood how the medication worked. It made me so exhausted, I didn't have the time to feel down or anxious. I hated it.

I also sleepwalked and talked in my sleep. When Chris told me I had demanded to sleep in a laundry basket, I didn't believe him. He showed me a picture and, sure enough, there I was in my pajamas hunched over in our laundry basket. My dear husband has a fun album on his phone called "Weird Places Esha Sleeps." Of course, he has shown it to a number of our friends. I fell asleep on my homework, holding a napkin at the dinner table, in the car, on the floor feeding Nala, and in many other places.

Chris was especially amused by my sleepwalking episodes. One night I got out of bed, stood at our closed bedroom window, and gave a speech. He said I must have dreamt I was Rosa Parks. These are two quotes he recalled for me:

"We will not use separate garbage cans"; "We are people and garbage is garbage."

When I went quiet, Chris walked me back to bed.

My younger cousin also witnessed one of these shining moments when she stayed the weekend in our first rental house. She and Chris were playing Uno. I went to bed, but didn't stay there. I walked from the bedroom to the kitchen and opened the window that faced the backyard. I don't know what it is about sleepwalking that draws me to windows.

When it came time to decide to end the medication or continue, I chose to end it. It took several months to start feeling like myself again, and I was occasionally still sleepwalking. I would try to handle this with talk therapy only.

Please know that medications work differently for everyone, so don't make a decision based on my experience. It's not the norm. Soon, I will tell you about more positive experiences I had with medications, including my current antidepressant and rescue pill. I am beyond grateful for both.

When in a depressed state, I had to push myself to shower. One day I stood naked in front of the bathtub. The water was on high and steam rolled through the room. For thirty minutes, I stood there thinking about getting in. I couldn't do it. I was remembering back in junior high, when I made up a song and sang it while I waited for the bus.

There's a single star in the sky. Just a single star. That star is me. That star is me. Got in a fight with some friends. Never thought it'd end. That star is me. That star is me.

As I stood there in the steam-filled room, I felt the loneliness and stress of that long-ago day overwhelm me. The song, I realized, was another missed sign of my depression. Chris came in to check on me, as he often did. I broke into tears and collapsed into him.

Time in the shower can be relaxing, rejuvenating and give you the best ideas. When you're dealing with depression, however, a shower can become your most vulnerable time of the day or week. You have access to razors, cleaning chemicals and towels. Even though I had no intention of misusing these items, the thoughts broke through and the images formed faster than I could rationalize. I'm so thankful I didn't do it, and I deeply sympathize with anyone who has. I mourn those who are gone and celebrate those who are still here.

I'm glad you're still here.

According to The Center for Disease Control and Prevention, "Suicide is the fourth leading cause of death for adults ages eighteen to sixty-five."[8] What a shockingly sad statistic. I spoke with Joe about my strange thoughts – the various things that came to mind and how much they scared me. Growing up, I thought suicide was the most selfish thing a person could do. I didn't want to die. I didn't want to do that to my family and friends. I wouldn't. I remember crying myself to sleep and reaching for a tissue. The tissue box was on Chris's nightstand. I had to reach over Chris and the 1911 handgun we keep for home defense.

To my great relief, Joe informed me that a person can have suicidal thoughts without being suicidal. He also said if he ever felt I was going to harm myself, he would intervene.

Oftentimes, I discussed my dreams with Joe. There had been recurring themes including being lost, chased, killed, mute, kidnapped, mutilated, and unable to walk or run to get away. Plenty of these dreams involved home invasion, car accidents, heavy traffic, and absence of the road beneath me. As you can imagine, I woke up with less energy and an assortment of moods.

No matter what I told him, Joe always validated my reality. More importantly, he taught me to listen to myself and look for red flags. Five years later, I still attend my counseling appointments. Long-term treatment is recommended for moderate or severe recurring depression and anxiety. Now my best friend goes to Joe

---

[8] Suicide Statistics and Facts https://save.org/about-suicide/suicide-facts/

for counseling. We're staying on track together. I usually go biweekly, but it might be more or less often depending on my schedule and stresses. I've come a long way. I'm glad I no longer deny myself care.

In the U.S., "80% to 90% of people who seek treatment for depression are treated successfully using therapy and/or medication."[9] If you are starting to lose faith that you'll get through this, I hope this fact from Save.org gives you hope.

It takes courage to go to therapy. It might take time to find a therapist that works well with you.

If you're uncomfortable being alone with someone of the opposite gender, it is okay to request a counselor of the same gender. When I was a little girl, I was afraid of almost all men. Thankfully, this fear did not carry into adulthood. Joe is an older man, and when I talk with him during my appointments it feels as natural as talking with a male family member.

Be sure to look into specialties. Mental health professionals specialize in numerous areas; for example, those who are certified in domestic violence counseling. If you're looking for a well-rounded counselor, search for "clinical mental health."

Additionally, it's important that your personalities and energy levels work well together. My counselor speaks in a soft tone and is laid back. That puts me at ease. My psychiatrist is closer to my age, she smiles a lot and I'm comfortable with her too. At both facilities, I completed an intake and was placed with someone the coordinator thought would be best for me. This could be helpful in determining the type of therapy you receive as well.

You might go to a few counseling sessions and realize it isn't working for you. Let the facility know. You might be referred to

---

[9] Suicide Statistics and Facts https://save.org/about-suicide/suicide-facts/

someone else in the building or someone better suited for you at a different location.

Muting Myths About Clinical Depression

As someone with depression, I've been called lazy. I've been told I feel tired or get upset for no reason. What's worse, I've also told myself these things. I believed it.

Let me reassure you. You're not being lazy. One of the symptoms of depression is fatigue. If you go outside the norm of your circadian rhythm, you feel more tired. It is true that you may sometimes have no valid reason to feel emotional. The chemical imbalance in your brain and changes in hormones don't know better. You're upset because your body is communicating those feelings to you.

As nice as it would be to be cured of this exhausting condition by smiling more or thinking happy thoughts, it doesn't work like that. Yes, there is a science to feeling better when you fake a smile. However, you won't be rid of depression or life stressors that may aggravate it. Depending on the severity and other factors, symptoms of depression can be lifelong. Don't let that discourage you. There are numerous ways to lessen those symptoms. The World Health Organization found that "up to 60% of people can recover with a proper combination of antidepressant drugs and psychotherapy."[10]

The next time someone tells you that you aren't trying hard enough to feel better, you can be rest assured that your pain and exhaustion are valid. You are trying and you are doing what is necessary to be okay.

---

[10] "World Health Organization." World Health Organization. NMH Communications, October 4, 2001. https://www.who.int/whr/2001/media_centre/press_release/en/.

Review and Reflect

Write three topics you would be willing to discuss with a provider or loved one.

Topic 1:

_____

_____

_____

_____

_____

_____

Topic 2:

_____

_____

_____

_____

_____

_____

Topic 3:

_____

_____

_____

_____

_____

_____

What would you want to gain from these conversations? What reservations might you have about opening up to another person?

_____

_____

_____

_____

_____

_____

_____

_____

_____

_____

_____

_____

_____

_____

_____

_____

_____

_____

_____

_____

_____

_____

_____

_____

_____

5

Recognizing Triggers and Trigger Symptoms

Pay attention to your triggers and trigger symptoms. I started learning about some of mine by asking myself questions like, "Why am I feeling down?" and "Why am I feeling anxious and scared?"

Social situations, health concerns, work meetings, personal and professional shortcomings, loneliness, certain sounds, large trucks driving behind me, driving under bridges, and even particular times of the day and night were triggers for me.

Joe recommended I get a Dialectic Behavioral Therapy (DBT) workbook. I started searching and was surprised to see how many DBT workbooks are available, including those for Borderline Personality Disorder, Anger Management, and Anxiety. I wound up buying two workbooks, one that taught the basics of mindfulness and emotion regulation, the other tailored to anxiety. I worked on the exercises and discussed what I learned during my appointments. I realized I could self-soothe, accept a circumstance for what it is and change how I react to it. The exercises were surprisingly simple and easy and brought about a tremendous change for me.

The workbook emphasizes the importance of distractions and

"avoiding avoidance."[11] I realized I'd been avoiding several things; for example, when something bothered me I tried to push it out of my thoughts. This worked for a short period of time, however, the uncomfortable situation still existed. I needed to acknowledge that. Instead of letting my discomfort consume me, I started to use DBT skills to help me reduce it. Afterward, I was able to return to the problem and handle it without judgment. This is key and one of the things the workbook repeatedly encourages readers to do.

One of the activities in the workbook was to create a "Distraction Plan."[12] It provided various skills one could use at home or away to bring about relaxation. I completed the activity in the workbook and copied my plan and skills to three index cards. For several months, I carried those cards in my purse and referred to the suggestions when necessary. Isn't it great when simple reminders can help you get through a rough day?

If you decide to add therapy workbooks to your mental health tools, here are some suggestions.

- Avoid skipping around in the workbook. (*I did this and noticed some of the lessons mentioned concepts from earlier chapters and I had to backtrack to find them.*)
- Read to comprehend. (*This is to absorb knowledge to use in your daily life.*)
- Allow yourself time to complete the activities.
- Be honest with yourself. This is to help you.

---

[11] McKay, Matthew, Jeffrey C. Wood, and Jeffrey Brantley. The Dialectical Behavior Therapy Skills Workbook: Practical DBT Exercises for Learning Mindfulness, Interpersonal Effectiveness, Emotion Regulation & Distress Tolerance. Oakland, CA: New Harbinger Publications, 2007.

[12] McKay, Matthew, Jeffrey C. Wood, and Jeffrey Brantley. The Dialectical Behavior Therapy Skills Workbook: Practical DBT Exercises for Learning Mindfulness, Interpersonal Effectiveness, Emotion Regulation & Distress Tolerance. Oakland, CA: New Harbinger Publications, 2007.

- Complete the activities in a place where you are comfortable and won't be interrupted.
- Read and work at your own pace.
- Practice your new skills.
- If you regularly see a mental health professional, discuss the concepts and activities with him/her.

I read an abstract from Behavior Research and Therapy on Science Direct. It was a fifty-six-week-long study on adding "mindfulness-based cognitive therapy" to standard treatment for patients with "at least three depressive episodes." The patients who received the mindfulness-based cognitive therapy "showed a significant reduction in both short- and longer-term depressive mood and better mood states and quality of life."[13]

I read quite a few posts on social media about people having elevated heart rates during panic attacks. As mentioned, I have an irregular heart rate and a heart murmur. My anxiety used to make it unbearable. I try to recognize my trigger symptoms before it gets out of control, then I'll focus on my breathing. If I become uncomfortably warm, I'll remove an outer layer of clothing and sip cold water, Gatorade, or fruit juice. My heartrate will return to normal after ten minutes. Sometimes, my arms and legs will continue to shake for thirty minutes to an hour.

I also had a strong emotional response to alcohol. Though I can't say for sure where this came from, I had lost a family member to a drunk driving accident; I was also afraid of someone from my

---

[13] K.A. Godfrin, C. van Heeringen

Corrigendum to "The effects of mindfulness-based cognitive therapy on recurrence of depressive episodes, mental health and quality of life: A randomized controlled study" [Behaviour Research and Therapy 48 (2010) 738–746]

Behaviour Research and Therapy, Volume 49, Issue 2, February 2011, Page 144.

dad's past who was controlled by wine. Were these factors enough to make me swear off alcohol in its entirety? At the time, it was. Also, it was not enough that I stayed away from alcohol – I wanted those I cared about to stay away from it too.

Having a mental illness didn't excuse the unforgivable things I said to my loved ones when they had beer or cocktails. My best friends reinforced that lesson. In my mind getting drunk was unacceptable. When I realized how unacceptable my own behavior was, I was truly mortified, especially since I had always considered myself a role model to my younger friend, cousins, and classmates.

Eventually, I became more self-aware and more careful with my words. The people who I'd hurt appreciated my efforts. This was not simply about changing my thoughts about an object; I changed the direction of the moral compass that had guided me my whole life. As you can imagine, this was not a small feat. There were two major turning points, both of which involved my adoring mother-in-law. The first was when she told me I would lose Chris if I tried to enforce limits and rules. At the time, I was considering asking him to drink non-alcoholic beers, no liquors, and not to go to events where alcohol was present. I'll discuss the other turning point, and my eventual growth, in later chapters.

I can't say what has most significantly reduced my depression and panic attacks. I was at different stages of self-awareness and treatment when I learned different coping skills and activities. Alternating those while I continued therapy and medications has been life-changing. Looking back, it's hard to believe I was adamant about declining both in the past, but that's okay. It was part of my process.

Now that I am true to myself and my needs, I fully understand how to control my emotions and lessen distress. I completed several mindful activities in my DBT workbook, then wrote a relaxation plan, a self-soothing plan and a distraction plan, all of which were personalized to my needs and my comfort. They were also adaptable depending on my environment and energy level.

If you're feeling like I was, and are ashamed of getting care for your mental health, please take small steps to come down safely from your high horse. Once you do this and start a personalized treatment plan, you'll feel more pride than you thought possible.

You won't need to make excuses to miss events. You won't need to apologize for your outbursts. You'll be in control. Yes, there will likely still be moments you can handle better. You'll learn from those.

Recognizing topics, environments, and people that trigger you will be a huge step in your progress.

Something that helps me during moments of panic, or helps me avoid them altogether, is remembering when I last felt that way. I was fearful, but I made it. I didn't get hurt or worse. Simple, yes, and it works for me. I've used it to calm friends too. When you take away the concerns of uncertainty and remind yourself that you've been through this or something similar and came out okay or stronger, you feel confident that you'll make it through this situation too. Sometimes, you need to convince the mind what *good* it can do.

Muting Myths About Anxiety Disorders

Though they have your best interests at heart, loved ones might underestimate your ability to keep plans and handle serious situations with composure.

For example, you might not be invited to parties because you've canceled at the last minute. Or maybe pertinent news is withheld from you because loved ones thought you couldn't handle it. I have experienced both, and as uncomfortable as it was I had to acknowledge my own role and take steps to change.

Now, instead of cancelling plans without warning, I try to stay in contact with the person planning the outing. I give status updates throughout the day so my friend or family member knows how I'm feeling and if I'm leaning toward going or staying home. Taking responsibility and showing consideration for another is a win, whether I attend or not. Next time you're feeling overwhelmed during the day and aren't sure you're up for going out, inform the host. Then, use your coping skills to try to achieve a better state of mind. If you still don't feel well enough, it's okay. You did what you could. Now you can rest and prepare for a better day tomorrow, knowing that you did the right thing by the other person.

The same is true when it comes to handling serious situations. People may have the impression that you need to be protected, perhaps because of the way you reacted to distressing news in the past. Different scenarios affect people differently, and living with an anxiety disorder doesn't mean you're less capable of under-standing. If you want honesty, let others know you're open to receiving it. Talk about your expectations and boundaries. Prepare yourself for the gut-wrenching pain that comes with such news.

Don't let anxiety disorders place limits on life's activities. Your company is appreciated and you deserve to be understood.

Review and Reflect

Think of two situations where you lost control of your emotions. You may find a trigger and/or a trigger symptom in these scenarios.

Scenario 1

What happened?

_____

_____

_____

_____

Who were you with?

_____

_____

_____

_____

What was said?

_____

_____

_____

_____

What physical symptoms did you experience?

_____

_____

_____

_____

Scenario 2

What happened?

_____

_____

_____

_____

Who were you with?

_____

_____

_____

_____

What was said?

_____

_____

_____

_____

What physical symptoms did you experience?

_____

_____

_____

_____

6

Taking the Fear Out of Medication

In 2015, the year following my initial diagnosis, I started taking an antidepressant. After a six-month trial period, I decided it wasn't right for me; I was also hesitant to try a different one. That first medication is what made me apathetic, fall asleep early in places other than my bed, and sleepwalk toward windows. I was determined to "power through" without medication. In 2017, I had a recurrence of depression. I sobbed at a joyous family event; the guilt over that lasted long after the tears had ended. My condition affected me at work too. I excused myself from meetings because of sadness, fatigue, self-doubt, and indecision. According to Save.org, depression is the leading cause of disability, worldwide.[14]

One day, I started crying uncontrollably at my desk and nearly hyperventilated. My wonderful work team heard me and pushed my computer chair into an office. In that moment, we formed our own support group. We talked about things we looked forward to and what made us happy.

At the time I had been seeing my counselor every other week and alternating with various coping activities. Realizing something had to change, I started making weekly counseling appointments.

---

[14] Suicide Statistics and Facts https://save.org/about-suicide/suicide-facts/

I also spoke to my primary care doctor about trying a new medication. When I told her about my experience with the first medication and my concern about going through that again, she suggested I take a GeneSite test. This test was fantastic! One painless cheek swab and a week later I had a list of medications that were likely to have the least, moderate, and most significant gene inter-action. I can't guarantee the test will yield accurate results for everyone, but it worked for me.

The next month, Jessica drove me to my intake appointment at the psychiatrist's office. She even showed me a route that allowed me to avoid the traffic circle. Those tend to make me nervous. I gave the psychiatrist my personalized list of medications, then Jessica and I headed to the local Dairy Queen. I ordered a "Reese's Treatza Pizza" and she ordered a "Blizzard." After my follow-up appointment, the psychiatrist prescribed medications that were likely to have the least amount of gene interaction. Easy peasy.

I began taking twenty milligrams of the antidepressant Trintellix and, after some initial grogginess, quickly adjusted to it. My psychiatrist also prescribed me vitamin B6 and instructed me to take it the week of my period. I noticed an immediate improvement in my energy and mood and asked to take it daily. After a couple of months of this regimen, I was feeling great. Coworkers, family and close friends told me they saw progress. That made me feel even better!

I also continued researching natural remedies on my own. One article on the health and wellness website LiveLoveFruit connected deficiencies of both Vitamin B6 and iron to panic disorder. The article was based on a Japanese study in which the sample patients, who went to the emergency room for panic attacks, were shown to be deficient in these nutrients. [15] I haven't added iron to my diet, or as a supplement, because I was doing so well with B6 and Trintellix.

Changing my perspective on medication was a game-changer. When my depression is under control, my anxiety is lower. When my anxiety is lower, I'm less likely to have a panic attack. This is good for my physical health as well, as panic attacks aggravate my irregular heart rate.

It's important to acknowledge the connection between mental health and physical health. In true moments of panic, I take my "rescue pill," Xanax. I used to feel weak and guilty when I took it; now I understand it's no different than needing a rescue inhaler. I wouldn't feel guilty about having asthma, so I shouldn't feel guilty for having panic disorder. I even personalized the pillbox. I added two strips of pink Post-it notes. I wrote "RESCUE ME" on the top and "Elicia Raprager" on the front. Ironically, I seldom need the rescue pill, because I regularly use my coping tools and always take my medication as prescribed.

Today, I'm thankful to have these medications working hard to treat me. They make it much easier for me to maintain my mental and physical wellbeing.

If you're starting a new medication, here are some tips:
- Write down the possible side effects.
- Keep a log of any side effects that you experience.
- Make an effort to take the medication at the same time each day (if it's for daily maintenance).

---

[15] Panic Attacks and Anxiety Linked To Low Vitamin B6 and Iron Levels

Carly Fraser - https://livelovefruit.com/panic-attacks-anxiety-linked-low-vitamin-b6-iron-levels/?fbclid=IwAR2GNaS-tDankZyHJIizNKDZ1k4nTahFmasnOFC1PVHgYRUma8FPu1ERoE4

- If you notice you're feeling worse, contact the prescribing physician immediately. You don't have to wait until your next appointment to address it.
- Most importantly, stay hopeful that you'll find a medication that works for you.

I hope this information helps you overcome any stigma you may feel about treating your mental health challenges. It can take some time to get things straightened out, but think of it this way: you've probably taken a similar, methodical approach when making a big purchase such as a car or a house.

Don't be discouraged if you suffer a setback. "The National Institute of Mental Health Consensus Development Conference on relapse and recurrence of depression found that 50% to 85% of people who have an episode of depression will suffer a recurrent episode during their lifetime. Of these, 50% will experience a recurrence within two years of the initial episode."[16]

Once, after a mix-up at the pharmacy, I was without my antidepressant for five days. I had been on the medication for almost two years at the time. I contacted my psychiatrist and let her know that I was unable to fill my prescription on time. On the sixth day, I would start my antidepressant again. I asked if I needed to cut the pill in half for the first few days, and was told that I did.

Being off my medication, even for such a short period, caused me to feel drowsy and less focused. Plus, readjusting to the medication gave me a slight headache. Stopping medication and readjusting to it is not something I want to do again. The point is that I got back on track and you will too, as long as you don't let

[16] Melfi CA, Chawla AJ, Croghan TW, Hanna MP, Kennedy S, Sredl K. The Effects of Adherence to Antidepressant Treatment Guidelines on Relapse and Recurrence of Depression. *Arch Gen Psychiatry.*1998;55(12):1128–1132. doi:10.1001/archpsyc.55.12.1128

negative stereotypes and past experiences with medications keep you from taking care of yourself. If talk therapy isn't enough to relieve your symptoms of depression and anxiety, speak with your physician about starting a medication regimen.

According to *Arch Gen Psychiatry*, "In this Medicaid system, premature discontinuation of antidepressant treatment was associated with a 77% increase in the risk of relapse/recurrence."[17]

Seeking Nature's Medicine

I ate handful after handful of Reese's Pieces while I searched for "savory vegetable recipes." I wrote a junk-food-shaming post about myself and requested quick, healthy eating tips. A vegetarian friend suggested I freeze a bag of seedless grapes for a refreshing treat, and I told her about my fear of finding a black widow spider in my grapes. I hadn't bought grapes since I read about that happening in Michigan. Yes, I worry about that. I apologize to my friend who now has that same fear.

An online friend told me to look into nutrition and how it impacts mood. I found on LiveLoveFruit that tryptophan contributes to serotonin production. A lack of serotonin impacts mood, memory, and sleep quality. Tryptophan is found in various vegetables and some fruits.[18] For a list of food sources of tryptophan, Vitamin B6, and iron, visit LiveLoveFruit.com. As always, please consult with your doctor before changing your diet or taking supplements. I only speak from my experiences, personal treat-

---

[17] *Ibid.*

[18] Panic Attacks and Anxiety Linked To Low Vitamin B6 and Iron Levels

Carly Fraser - https://livelovefruit.com/panic-attacks-anxiety-linked-low-vitamin-b6-iron-levels/?fbclid=IwAR2GNaS-tDankZyHJIizNKDZ1k4nTahFmasnOFC1PVHgYRUma8FPu1ERoE4

ment, and research. I am not a medical or mental health professional.

I had been wanting to eat healthier for a while, plus Chris had been trying to lose weight. I tried to add more vegetables to our diet. I watched videos on how to cut zucchini into noodles. I chose ground turkey instead of ground beef. To cut out carbs, we had garlic pita chips instead of garlic toast. I forgot to check if zucchini needed to be refrigerated. When I took it out of the bag, the sour smell told me the answer. The middle was still firm, but the ends were mushy and ashy gray.

The vegetable peeler made the strips as thin as chips – nothing like the slices in the videos. Being concerned about the smell and the lack of noodle thickness, I tossed it. Next time, I'll refrigerate the zucchini. I might also look into getting a vegetable spiralizer, which was recommended to me by a few friends who enjoy their healthy "zoodles."

Clearly I needed a simpler addition for our new healthy meals. Jessica made us fantastic veggie tots in her air fryer. They tasted like the ones my Grandma P used to order at a restaurant she frequented. *Those can't be too difficult,* I thought. I bought some sweet potato and broccoli veggie tots and baked those. Mine must have been a different brand, because the consistency was less like a tot and more of a nauseating paste. The taste was unpleasant too. Chris and I finished the bag but we never bought them again.

Like anything, I can't expect to get it right the first time. We had some pretty awful meals during this learning period. We ate a lot of processed foods afterward. Soon enough, though, we got back on track. I got in the habit of buying frozen vegetables. They lasted longer and didn't require cutting. I challenged myself to use the slow cooker more. It was healthy and convenient, especially since I work from home. I prepare the ingredients on my first break and throw it in the crockpot during my lunch. Making small changes such as cooking healthier meals has helped me feel better about myself and keep anxiety at bay.

Review and Reflect

What concerns do you have when it comes to treating your mental health conditions?

_____

_____

_____

_____

_____

_____

_____

_____

_____

_____

_____

_____

_____

_____

_____

_____

_____

_____

Use the space below to write a conversation you would like to have about treating your mental health conditions.

Consider who you're speaking with, the time of day, and location. Feel free to use your topics from Chapter 4's Review and Reflect.

_____

_____

_____

_____

_____

_____

_____

_____

_____

_____

_____

_____

_____

_____

_____

_____

_____

_____

_____

7

Do I Have Schizophrenia?

In this chapter you'll see how our assumptions, born of fear and panic, are often worse than reality.

I wanted to be as quiet as possible. I also wanted to open the door quickly, like ripping off a bandage.

"Mom, I'm so scared." I whispered.

"Elicia, I can't hear you. Speak up."

"I can't. I think someone is inside the house. I heard movement outside. A few minutes ago, there was a loud noise in the living room. Nala heard it too. She jumped and growled."

My face and body grew hot. I thought about grabbing the handgun. My eyes were flooded with panicked tears. My body was trembling. I knew I wouldn't be able to aim. Chris was staying with friends out of state and I had been alone all week. He was coming home that day, but what if it was too late?

"Esha, hang up and call the police."

With a shaking hand I did as I was told.

"Nine-one-one, what's your emergency?"

"I-I'm home alone and I think s-someone just broke in. I heard a loud noise and it startled my cat."

Two police officers reported to my front door. The dispatcher stayed on the phone with me and told me I needed to let the officers inside. I told her I was afraid to leave my bedroom.

"Your door is locked. The officers are unable to enter."

I peeked outside and saw a glimpse of one of the uniforms. I took a deep breath. My heart was running in place as I opened the bedroom door. I saw no one in the hall. There was no one in the living room. I unlocked the front door and the screen door.

The officers came in and looked around, finding nothing. One of them pointed out the solid locks on my house. They checked all the windows and confirmed those were locked too. People are lazy, he said. If someone wanted in my house, they would try my door first, then move to a window. If the window didn't open, that person would most likely move to a different house or vehicle. He was trying to comfort me, but I was ashamed.

After Chris left for his trip, I had moved the trash can, snacks, my coloring books, journal, and everything else I needed into the living room. Other than to sleep, I was *living* in the living room. I was fearful of going to the back of the house. I couldn't see if anyone came to the door or hear if anyone knocked. I was in my pajamas and my hair was unwashed and snarled. And the police officers had just witnessed *all* of it.

I was concerned about my well-being and possibly my sanity. I scheduled an appointment with a psychiatrist, who recommended that I participate in a psychological screening. The screening was expensive, and not covered because it was performed by an out-of-network technician. If you have this done, I recommend you search for someone within your network.

I was warned beforehand that it would take a long time – between two and three hours – but I was able to get it done within a shorter period, probably because of the inner work I had been doing. The key is to be honest with yourself and not second-guess your answers and I didn't have a problem with that. Once I was done with the computer assessments, I went into a room with a technician. She held up pictures, diagrams, and patterns for me to solve, and presented the cognitive puzzles with limited instructions. It was kind of fun, but I felt a little stressed. I said my thought pattern out loud to prove to myself and the technician that I was logical. I was hoping the test would relieve me of any worry about being diagnosed with psychosis.

I was also concerned about having schizophrenia because of the thoughts, dreams, and paranoia I had experienced over the years. In a training at work, we had watched a TED Talk about schizophrenia and how this condition is often misunderstood. The speaker was intelligent and held a high position in her career; she also suffered from, and had to be institutionalized for, schizophrenia. She talked about how staff members slammed her frail body onto a hard table and strapped her to it; how she felt like less of a person. I was grateful to this woman for bringing awareness to this issue; it also gave me hope to hear that she was still employed and played an important role in her field. Most importantly, I learned that letting depression and anxiety go untreated can potentially result in schizophrenia. It's more common in women, who usually begin to show symptoms in their mid-to-late twenties.[19] My age, gender and lack of treatment in the past qualified me for this risk. I had denied that I needed counseling and medication several times.

When I received the screening results, I learned I am indeed at moderate risk of developing schizophrenia. I'm not too concerned about it though, because I'm being treated for my MDD and panic disorder. I was also tested for Bipolar 2, or "bipolar light," that day and thankfully, I did not have that either. The thought of losing

---

[19] Saks, Elyn. "YouTube." YouTube (blog). TedTalks, July 2, 2012.
https://www.youtube.com/watch?v=f6CILJA110Y.

impulse control scares me. I'm disciplined by nature and care about my reputation as a straight-edge person.

When Fear Had Control

As I've shared throughout this book, I used to be controlled by fear. For example, I worried that a large truck would rear-end me on the expressway or that someone walking on the overpass would jump and land on the windshield of my car. Also, I worried about overpasses breaking and crushing my car with me inside.

I worried that someone was watching and judging me as I stayed in pajamas all day. I worried that someone would come into my home and hurt me. I saw myself being shot, stabbed, raped, or jumping off a building. I was scared of the building I worked in being bombed or planes flying into it. To me, these were schizo-phrenic thoughts, which brought on a whole new set of fears. With Joe's help, I learned how to control this thinking. I did it by con-sidering the likeliness (or rather, unlikeliness) of the scary event. Eventually, I began to see how my fear was much more likely to cause my demise than anything else.

I remember finding a spider in my vehicle on my way home from the Flint campus. I called my mom and told her about it. She told me not to crash, that if I were to lose my life over a spider I wouldn't graduate from college or make it to my wedding day. Those were powerful words. The wedding was only a couple months away. I watched the spider come down from my visor to my passenger window, up my window, above my head, and back onto the window. I rolled it down and the spider rolled down with it. Then, after a few minutes of hanging out in the crevice of the window track, it went outside and I rolled the window back up. I was safe.

One weekend several years later, I visited my mom. When it was time to leave I headed out to my car and was surprised to see the driver's side window was rolled down. There was a thin line of web running down the length.

"No! Please don't let there be any spiders in my car!"

That previous car ride, and my mother's words, flashed through my mind. I had made it to graduation and I had made it to my wedding day. Now, if I were to get in a wreck, I wouldn't reach another significant goal: finishing my book. The whole way home I kept an eye out for a spindly hitchhiker but, thankfully, it seemed I was alone.

Another time, as I was heading to visit my mom and stepdad, I was overcome by sadness and started to sob. About ten miles from Mom's house I got off the expressway and pulled into the parking lot of a random small business. I cried, wiped my eyes and let my mom know I was off the road. She reminded me to breathe. She asked me if I needed to call Joe. I let her know I was fine, that I had suddenly felt sad. I had parked the car so I could cry without endangering my or others' safety.

While dealing with some unfortunate stressors, one of which was a lawsuit, I had become a little paranoid. The front door on our second rental house had three windows, the lowest close to the door handle. While the lawsuit was going on, someone broke into my car and I was also nervous about being watched. Thankfully, the fact that we were renting the house kept me from acting too rashly. I took sheets of wax paper and covered the two lower windows. This only made things harder, though, because with the windows covered I couldn't tell who was at the door. Eventually, the wax paper had rips in it large enough to peak through and I removed it.

Then, about a month before we moved to our first purchased

home, there was a young male lurking about. He attempted to break into cars on our street and snuck into backyards. Chris and I invested in security cameras that were accessible on our phones and computers. We captured his moves and sent the footage to the local police department. This helped me feel much better.

I no longer allow fear to rule me in my home. I feel safe and have control over intrusive thoughts. I open the curtains and blinds each morning to let in the daylight. I close them when it starts to get dark.

The therapy workbooks were instrumental in helping me deal with my fears. I kept them by the loveseat, the spot where I often used to get "stuck." Especially helpful was an exercise in the "Advanced Distress Tolerance Skills" chapter.[20] The exercise was to think of or create a place that brought you comfort and made you feel calm. It's a breathing exercise too. I counted breaths and used my five senses to immerse myself in my second childhood home.

I could see the dining room table with my mom's artwork on it. I could smell baked goods in the oven. I could hear Mom singing Ty Herndon's "Hat Full of Rain" and Mark watching a Sci-Fi show. I felt my mom's hug and her laying a blanket over me on the loveseat. I tasted a roast beef dinner with soft mashed potatoes and my favorite gooey oatmeal chocolate chip cookies. I was at my home away from home. Minutes before, I'd been crying on the couch and feeling like a hopeless failure. Now, this simple exercise had helped me feel comfortable and loved. All I needed was fifteen to twenty minutes in a quiet room without distractions.

The beauty of this exercise is that you can do it as many times as you need to. Sometimes it might be difficult to find your safe

---

[20] McKay, Matthew, Jeffrey C. Wood, and Jeffrey Brantley. The Dialectical Behavior Therapy Skills Workbook: Practical DBT Exercises for Learning Mindfulness, Interpersonal Effectiveness, Emotion Regulation & Distress Tolerance. Oakland, CA: New Harbinger Publications, 2007.

space; other times it might be easy. You might see or hear different sights and sounds each time. When I was alone and missing my late Grandma P, I returned to my safe space. This time, I did my best to place my grandma there.

"Hello, Elicia Marie, you skinny little turd. I love you, sweetheart. I brought you one of those flavored waters and 'pe-fume.' Remember to take it with you when you go home."

"I love you, Grandma. Thank you."

I skipped to sitting at the crowded dinner table. Grandma would be telling us a story about a family member. Maybe, we would be poking fun at her use of landmarks when giving directions.

This exercise helped for a few minutes, but when I opened my eyes I was back to missing her. I held her picture and expressed my love and sorrow. My glasses caught my tears. I reminded myself that grief is a different type of pain, one everyone feels and needs to release at some point. It comes in waves and it's okay to feel her absence.

Review and Reflect

What helps you feel safe when you're suddenly panicked?

_____

_____

_____

_____

_____

_____

If you use calming affirmations, write those in the space below.

_____

_____

_____

_____

_____

_____

_____

_____

_____

_____

_____

_____

_____

_____

_____

_____

_____

_____

_____

PART THREE

Self-Care and Personal Development

These are two amazing phases. You dedicate months, a year, or longer to loving yourself and making your dreams become a reality. Although your workload is immeasurable, you'll appreciate your self-worth and be proud of the person you're becoming.

You'll begin to enjoy leisure time and learn what activities, places, and people are good for you. You'll limit time on anything that drains you or triggers panic attacks or depressive episodes. This is the beginning of your transformation into the new, better you.

Here are some things to remember when embracing self-care:
- Self-care is not selfish.
- Set boundaries.
- Set a schedule.
- Rotate your activities and consider the energy level required for each.
- Eat a healthy diet.
- Recharge as needed.

Here are some ways family and friends can support your need for self-care:

- Suggest self-care activities when you're bored or feeling low.
- Be understanding of boundaries.
- Remind you not to take on too much at once.
- Understand the benefits of a self-care routine.
- Offer to join in on a relaxing activity.

"In dealing with those who are undergoing great suffering, if you feel 'burnout' setting in, if you feel demoralized and exhausted, it is best, for the sake of everyone, to withdraw and restore yourself. The point is to have a long-term perspective."
~ Dalai Lama[21]

Once you've established a self-care routine and started feeling the benefits from it, you may want to consider expanding your efforts into personal development.

This is where you start to think about what you want in life. Your passion for goals grows. The best version of yourself is being carefully sculpted. Think about your childhood dreams. What did you want to be when you grew up? Is there still truth in that today?

Here are some things to think about when embracing personal development:
- Investments in yourself and your future are priceless.
- Nurture your strengths and (lovingly) understand your weaknesses.
- Dream big, but start small.

---

[21] "Dalai Lama." AZQuotes.com. Wind and Fly LTD, 2020. 31 January 2020. https://www.azquotes.com/quote/543315

- Write a detailed plan with manageable steps to accomplish your goal.
- Share your goals with trusted family and friends.
- Surround yourself with like-minded people.

Here are some ways family and friends can assist you in achieving your goals:

- Inform you of possible opportunities.
- Ask about your progress in achieving goals.
- When you're discouraged, remind you of your accomplishments and the steps you've taken to achieve the goal.
- Remind you why it's important to invest time and money into growth.
- Help you maintain focus.

In the following chapters, you will read about my efforts to prioritize self-care, recover from a break in my routine, and find my purpose.

Like success in work and school, ongoing personal growth is significant to your mental health and well-being. I discovered my love for writing at an early age. In my twenties, I realized I could use that to help others through their struggles with depression and anxiety, and to spread much-needed joy on social media. These things have come to mean a lot to me. Can you envision your future self? Are you ready to meet the new you? You've earned it.

"Nourishing yourself in a way that helps you blossom
in the direction you want to go is attainable,
and you are worth the effort."
~ Deborah Day[22]

---

[22] Popular Quotes By Deborah Day https://allauthor.com/quotes/author/deborah-day/

8

One Size Doesn't Fit All:
Self-Care is Personalized

Chris jokes that I'm simultaneously eight and eighty years old. There is truth in his claim. What comforted me as a child still comforts me today. When I visit my mom, I'll sometimes rest my head on her lap and she runs her fingers through my hair. It reminds me of when my paternal grandpa calmed me during a scary movie. I sat on his lap and he gently rubbed my back from side to side until I nodded off.

Below is my list of self-care tools. It's quite lengthy, but I assure you that at one point or another I have received assistance from each of them.
- Seasonal Affective Disorder therapy (SAD) lamp
- Personal journal
- Coloring books for adults
- Colored pencils
- Happiness Planner
- Kindle Paperwhite
- Therapy workbooks
- Personal Strengths and Weaknesses
- Yoga mat for meditation
- Soft blanket

- Weighted blanket
- Comfort teas
- Favorite mug
- Comfort movies
- Paint pallet
- Jewelry (hobby) book
- Hobby journal
- Talking pen
- Medications
- Reminder cards for counseling appointments
- Physical fitness equipment
- Calming lavender body wash
- Chocolate (comfort food)
- Essential Oils diffuser
- Bed for resting my tired thoughts
- Nala, my little sweetheart

You too may need a combination of self-care techniques and activities. If you've tried one or two methods without success, do some research and find some more. Some days, you may need to alternate between several techniques. Other days, you may need just one or two, or none at all. The important thing is to be kind to yourself, each and every day.

I still have challenging days. One weekend morning, I didn't feel well enough to go to the gym and instead laid awake in bed until nine thirty-five a.m. It was hard to acknowledge the struggle without judging myself. It was a difficult weekend, but I moved forward. You can do the same.

Take time for yourself. Talk with others and share self-care techniques. When people see my progress, they ask me what has helped me the most. Again, it's not one thing. I was at different places in my treatment when I picked up various coping skills and activities. Regular counseling, medication and leisure time have been significant for me. It's not about one being better than the other. It's about figuring out what works for you and alternating those coping techniques. Establishing a routine has also been essential. I like to know when things are going to happen, how long, and how frequently.

Being in control and having a plan relieves me of anxiety. It makes me more accountable too. While having a routine is important, it's just as important not to beat yourself up when you break it. We're human. It happens. Learn from all experiences. I've learned it's better to be kind and forgiving. It's better to learn. That's what promotes growth. Please don't make yourself a toxic character in your story. Anxiety and Depression have already filled those roles.

I've mentioned several coping activities that I use. If you find some that suit you well, keep track of them so you can use them later. This is a toolkit that will mend and recharge you. It needs to be accessible and versatile. On days when I feel tired and unmotivated, I'll choose coping activities that require the least energy. These could be meditating, coloring or sipping on a hot beverage, all of which are simple and calming. I can do them while lying down or sitting. Well, I should probably sit up to drink the hot beverage. Spilled hot tea is a stressor I don't need.

Think about your different days and weeks. There are days where I am perky and inspired from sunup to sundown. Other days, I stay in bed as long as I can before I risk being late for work or an appointment and go to bed early at night. Most days, I have enough energy to do one or more productive tasks. On those days, I'll exercise vigorously for thirty minutes, call a family member who makes me feel loved, or complete a mindfulness activity in my therapy workbooks. Self-care is personalized. What works today may not work as well tomorrow or the next day. My medium-energy coping activities are grounding, journaling and reflection, and positive affirmations.

Getting back to your passion can be an enormous act of self-care. I made a calendar on a dry erase board and color-coded my hobbies and self-care activities. When I went months without drawing or painting, I felt something was missing. I was less myself. Once I resumed those activities, my creative energy returned and fueled me throughout the day. It was an awakening feeling. I told myself I was going to write and work on my creative projects weekly and exercise three days a week. For a while I did, then work, family obligations, studying and other factors once again got in the way.

Break down the barriers. I'm working long hours. What other times can I go to the gym? My sweet intake has been high. What else can I eat? Family obligations don't fit into my busy schedule. What can I move to another week so I can make family a priority? I was hard on myself. That's a theme with mental health survivors and creative people. We are our worst critics.

One of the best purchases I made was my SAD (seasonal affective disorder) therapy lamp. It is especially useful during the winter months, when there is much less daylight, which is our greatest source of mood-boosting vitamin D. When my psychiatrist first suggested the lamp I was skeptical, but thankfully decided to take her advice. Within just two weeks it started to make a noticeable difference. Now I use it three hundred sixty-five days a year.

I start most days by sitting in front of my SAD lamp from one to two hours (I work from home, so this is doable for me). During this time, I also eat breakfast and take my pills. On gym days, I eat a small breakfast and take my pills before heading out. The lamp goes on after I've showered and clocked into work.

Recently, I was struggling with sleep more than usual. As I was also recovering from a mild illness, getting quality sleep was especially important. After being awake for two days straight, I decided it was time to purchase a weighted blanket. I had looked into them in the past but the cost deterred me. Now, thanks to some gift cards, I was able to purchase a fifteen-pound blanket for twenty-two dollars! If you are considering one, be sure to check out the size charts to make sure you get one appropriate for your height and weight. They also come in different fabrics for hot and cold sleepers. I went with the basic fabric. It was an unusually warm fall, so I used a ceiling fan to regulate my body temperature. Find what's right for you.

The day it was delivered, I laid down with it after work and fell asleep in about an hour. I was out for two hours, though it probably would have been longer if that "Scam Likely" call hadn't woken me up. In the product warning, I had read that it can take two to seven days to adjust to a weighted blanket. I had also been warned by a friend that I might feel some neck and shoulder soreness the first few times. Thankfully, neither was true for me. I was comfortable with it from day one and didn't feel any of the soreness my friend mentioned.

The next day, I searched for a sleep mask to block the light. The blanket felt like a comforting embrace; the mask prevented me from looking around the room when my mind was active. Sometimes I also listen to a guided meditation to quiet my thoughts before bed.

I find the "Leaves on a Stream" meditation,[23] which can be found on the Insight Timer and Mindfulness Muse applications,

---

[23] Insight Network Inc, (2010) Insight Timer - Free Meditation App (14.1.4) [Google Play Store].

particularly helpful. You lightly close your eyes and imagine watching a stream. Leaves float down the stream. As thoughts pop into your mind, you observe them, then set them on the leaf and watch them float away downstream. It doesn't matter whether a thought is pleasing, exciting, concerning or frustrating – you follow the same process. It's an effective method to clear the mind.

Though meditation may seem effortless, it takes practice. In fact, it may be quite some time before you are able to let go of intrusive thoughts. Don't let this discourage you. It's called a mindfulness *practice* for a reason.

When I was having trouble at work and couldn't focus on a task long enough to complete it, I started doing "mind dumps." I would take five or ten minutes and write everything on my mind. What was concerning me? What was I looking forward to? What did I have to do later that day? When I did this, it made it easier for me to concentrate. Sometimes I needed to do this a second time later in the day, but it has consistently helped. I've also suggested this to friends I noticed were struggling to complete a task. I'm not sure if there is a technical term for it, or who first thought of it. The idea came to me when I needed it and I still use it today.

Nala, my cat, is not a registered support animal, but her presence in the home comforts me. When I rest, she joins me. Most of the time, she sticks by my side when I'm upset. Only once did she make me feel worse. I was crying in the living room. I got off the loveseat and kneeled on the floor. I laid my head on a chair next to Nala. It must have bothered her, because after several minutes of watching me dab my eyes and nose with tissues she jumped down from the chair and left the room. She left me when I needed her, which shows she's not trained to provide emotional support. For the most part, though, she behaves like a pro.

Support animals can detect various behavioral and medical

episodes. They can warn a person not to exert him or herself. They can stop a person from leaving the house, or performing an act of self-harm. Also, support animals can put a distressed person at ease. There are legal processes to follow to register your pet as a support animal. If you want to do this, please familiarize yourself with the process so no one is harmed.

One night Chris found me on the loveseat coloring. Nala was nestled at my side. It was Christmas week, and the Yuletide fireplace played on the television and our Christmas tree lights twinkled. I sipped on hot cocoa and listened to the recorded fire crack and pop.

"How old are we?" Chris teased.

I stuck out my tongue and blew a kiss.

On the other hand, I get annoyed by some of the same behaviors that the elderly typically find to be a nuisance. After the neighborhood kids ding-dong-ditched us for the fourth time, I swung open the front door and yelled, "Go read a book!"

My husband rang in, "I see old lady Esha is back."

"Haha, very funny," I said, but even I could see the humor in it.

Break Larger Chores into Manageable Tasks

Regular mental health maintenance is critical. I've seen some lighthearted memes on social media comparing human beings to flowers and houseplants. The memes describe people as being capable but dehydrated and having a range of complicated emotions. Last year when Chris and I returned home from our summer vacation, the metaphor became more apparent.

My flowers had been flourishing before our trip. However, while we were gone they had endured consecutive days of high heat indexes, only to be hit with prolonged heavy rainfall the night of our return.

Our street and parts of the neighborhood flooded, so we had to park down the road and make three trips from our car to the house. I tied my tennis shoes to my beltloop and wore my sandals, which quickly became saturated. When we got inside, Chris checked the basement. It was mostly dry. Only the furnace room had some water and it was thankfully minimal.

When the water receded, I noticed six-inch tall weeds in my flower beds. Some flowers remained bright and upright. Others looked unwell, to put it kindly. The flowerbed behind the house I had cleared now had weeds covering the entire surface. Being tired and knowing the yardwork would take longer due to my break from it, I put it off. A week later, when I tackled the task, the weeds had grown out of control. Their pointy defenses were strong. They did not easily uproot.

Similarly, if you put off going to appointments or doing your self-care activities, your conditions might get the best of you, like the nuisance weeds got the best of my yard and garden.

I took back my yard, breaking the chores down into manageable chunks. I set an alarm on my lunch break and mowed for twenty minutes. I mowed a third of the small yard in that amount of time. After work, I mowed the rest. The next day, I weed whacked and pulled weeds.

The flower beds weren't as clean as they could be, but those sections needed only a little more effort after that. You can think similarly about your own well-being. If you weren't able to make it to therapy or refill your medications, you might struggle to reschedule or drive to the pharmacy. If you spread these tasks out over a couple days, it seems less daunting. My counselor frequently reminds me to do things one at a time. I am a multitasker. When

I'm outside of business hours, I try to keep multitasking to a minimum. This keeps my day organized and manageable.

My mood therapy lamp supports my energy level, improves my mood, and maintains a steady circadian rhythm. Like any product or treatment, there are potential side effects. The manufacturer warns to discontinue or lessen use if you feel jittery afterward. As mentioned, I use the lamp (on the highest setting) for one to two hours each morning; occasionally, I use it for thirty minutes in the afternoon too. I have not felt jittery or had any trouble from daily use. If you purchase a mood therapy lamp, I suggest thoroughly reading the directions and warnings. I have my lamp set twenty-four inches away facing my left side. I only use it in a brightly lit room. I never use it five hours before bed. I'm a stickler for following rules. I am an auditor, after all.

One of my friends was concerned about the bright light doing damage to my eyes. I wear transition glasses, which means the lenses tint when I go out in the sun to protect my eyes. Following my friend's concern, I placed my transition glasses in front of the lamp and left the room for ten to fifteen minutes. I came back and the lenses had not darkened. This demonstrated that ultraviolet rays were not harming my eyes when using the lamp.

I do feel withdrawals when I go on vacation and leave the lamp behind. I don't get headaches or feel ill, but the fatigue associated with depression and anxiety slowly returns. It takes me about seven days of use to feel energized again.

The lamp also works on my peace lily, which I brought home from a funeral in November. I watered it regularly but the flowers were turning brown and the leaves were wilting. It wasn't getting enough sunlight. I sat the plant in front of my SAD lamp and rotated it every thirty minutes or longer so each side could absorb it. The plant started to do much better. Even in the winter months, it got the daylight it needed.

I regularly see my counselor and psychiatrist. I take my medications as prescribed and prioritize self-care. I am getting back into an exercise routine, which helps me burn off anxious energy and sleep better. I journal to give myself an outlet and process my thoughts. Also, I try to talk with or visit family or friends once a week. This helps me because I'm a homebody. When I notice my anxiety or depression is increasing, I make more frequent appointments and try to minimize my to-do list so it doesn't add to the overwhelming feelings I sometimes get. I try to be honest with myself and set aside blame.

Review and Reflect

What three coping activities would you like to try?

Coping Activity 1:

_____

_____

_____

_____

Coping Activity 2:

_____

_____

_____

_____

Coping Activity 3:

_____

_____

_____

_____

How do you rate your average energy level?

_____

_____

_____

_____

_____

_____

_____

_____

What routine would you like to start?

_____

_____

_____

_____

_____

_____

_____

_____

_____

_____

How will you start it?

_____

_____

_____

_____

_____

_____

_____

_____

_____

_____

_____

9

Overcoming My Fear of Alcohol

I haven't been diagnosed with Obsessive Compulsive Disorder (OCD), but I used to be consumed by obsessive thoughts. My persistent concerns with others' alcohol consumption began to hurt my relationship with Chris, as well as my most cherished friendships. This chapter illustrates how irritable, irrational, and inconsolable depression and anxiety can make a person.

At a young age, I developed strong, negative feelings about alcohol. When I met and married Chris, he didn't drink, a wonderful rarity in our peer group. We were sober and happy at parties. I felt our sobriety was something that helped us become a compatible couple. One day, my husband went to the Renaissance Festival with his buddies. When he returned, I learned that he had also gone to a pub crawl and sampled several meads, an alcoholic drink created by fermenting honey.

As Chris proudly showed me his badges and souvenirs from the crawl, I became distraught and irrationally angry. That same night, I wrote a list of rules and statements to remember when he drinks. It was biased toward me and riddled with my hasty assumptions. I tried to find the list to include in this chapter, but I think I threw it out, no doubt out of shame at how I used to think.

Here is a particularly upsetting memory from 2017. Chris, a mutual friend and I visited Ashley and her husband, other friends who lived out of state. While we were in the kitchen, Chris opened a Leinenkugel Summer Shandy and started drinking it. I asked him what he was doing.

He simply stated the obvious. "I'm having a beer."

Until that moment, Chris had not had any alcohol in front of me. In fact, I didn't even think he'd had a drink since that terrible pub crawl. I walked into the living room to watch movies with Ashley while he and some others stayed in the kitchen and played boardgames. I watched in disbelief as my husband went to the fridge three times, each time grabbing a Summer Shandy. Four beers in three hours! I had heart palpitations and cried hot tears. My hands, legs and feet trembled too. Ashley, who happens to be a counselor as well as dear friend, tried to comfort me.

I texted my husband and begged him to switch to tea or water. He didn't deny or offer any explanation about his behavior. I went upstairs to bed, where I sent Chris a series of cruel, profane texts describing what I hoped would happen to him after drinking that much. In my mind, he needed to feel the consequences of his actions. Later he read the text messages and was justifiably upset. He explained to me that he'd only had one beer. He grabbed the other three for our friends because he was sitting closest to the fridge. I apologized and told him how uncomfortable the thought of him drinking made me. It didn't matter. My angry words were too much to set aside.

At the time, I didn't know how to cope with alcohol entering my husband's life. The irritability associated with anxiety and depression had gotten the best of me. My close friends remind me of this when I feel guilty about the way I behaved. Having their support was like falling from a tightrope and knowing they'd catch me.

In July of that summer, my husband and I, along with the same buddy, visited my in-laws in Wisconsin. We had just finished lunch and were sitting around the bonfire. A family member took a sip of a Pepsi Fire and dumped it out.

He said it tasted like "weak-ass Fireball," then asked Chris if he'd ever had Fireball whiskey.

Nonchalantly, Chris replied, "Yeah, I've had Fireball."

I walked away, heartbroken, disappointed and infuriated. I was inconsolable. That unbearable, heavy-hearted feeling would last through September. I spoke with my closest friends, family members, family doctor, counselor and husband. It took a long time, but I realized Chris hadn't done anything wrong. Yes, he could have told me that he continued to drink after the pub crawl so it wasn't such a shock. That's not the point. Chris was responsible and hadn't changed like I feared he would. Joe suggested I try visualizations to trick my mind. He suggested walking in a store with alcohol in my cart and practicing mindfulness. This advice was appreciated and followed, though I told everyone who glanced at me that I wasn't going to buy it.

What I found most helpful, however, was something I did on my own. I wrote a list of reasons why alcohol bothered me and brainstormed what I could do to lessen my heated reactions to it.

When I showed the list to my friends, Sandra suggested I write instances when I was okay being around alcohol. That was helpful too. I was surprised to think of as many examples as I did.

That July trip was like trying to ignore a massive sign with flashing lights. I imagined the words on that sign read: DIVORCE, LONELINESS, DEATH.

I love and appreciate my husband and friends and did not want to continue resenting them for these situations that sprung up. To help me realize what I have and reassure myself that I needed to be more accepting, I wrote a lengthy list of all the things that I love about Chris. It was easy. I didn't want to lose him.

I realized drinking does not change Chris. He's still the charismatic guy I fell in love with in 2009. He's still the funny, sweet guy I married in 2012. He's still my loving, goofy and reliable husband and cat dad. Plus, his drinking has not made us less of a couple. Overcoming this obstacle made our marriage stronger.

In 2018, Chris and I once again stayed with my wonderful in-laws, this time to celebrate the Fourth of July. They told me it was good to see me doing so well. On the Fourth we went to a bar/restaurant. It was just before dusk. The place was loud. A few people were inebriated. There were four young children present and some women were wearing bikini tops and skimpy shorts. That got to me. I was on edge for the first fifteen minutes. I told Chris and my in-laws that I needed to get it out of my system and I would be fine.

Chris wanted to order an Apple Ale, and I decided I would take a sip and bond with him. Turns out I was off the hook because the waitress didn't return to our table until he had eaten most of his burger. I ate a delicious pulled pork barbeque sandwich. My funny father-in-law joked that he could see my review.

"The food was great, but the people were obnoxious," I laughed in agreement.

I prefer to post reviews when I receive excellent customer service. My blog post titled, "Eye Laughed Away My Stress" is a light-hearted narrative of my delayed but great appointment with the eye doctor.

It's been a long road, but I am no longer sent into an episode by the mention of "Fireball," my husband drinking in front of me, or having alcohol in our home.

In August of 2018, Ashley and her husband returned the visit. As they settled in, Chris asked if I would mind if they went out and bought drinks. I said no.

"By drinks, you know I mean beer, right?"

I nodded and said yes. Chris thanked me and gave me a kiss. He offered to bring home a wine for me to try. I told him I had been thinking about it and felt ready. Previously, I had spoken with my psychiatrist about having an occasional drink. I read the warning labels on my medication and read more on the drug manufacturer's website. My antidepressant had been working so well and I didn't want my progress to be ruined by a little wine. Ashley also helped me feel more comfortable.

I announced that at seven-thirty that evening, I would try the wine. I envisioned a momentous milestone and even thought about "going live" for the first time on social media to capture the moment. I considered inviting Jessica and Sandra who have helped me (mostly) overcome this ridiculous phobia.

I did none of that. I told myself this was daily living for millions of people. I needed to get over myself. While we played games, our friends had beer and red wine. It may have been my nose, but the beer smelled like a public bathroom that had been cleaned with lemon scented products. I barely smelled the red wine.

As seven-thirty approached, Chris poured me a glass of the supposedly sweetest white wine.

"Here you go, sweetie."

I let it sit for a few minutes, and Chris reminded me that it tastes better cold. After about ten minutes, I picked up the glass. It smelled fruity. That was a good sign. I looked at Chris and our friends. We clinked glasses.

"To being open-minded," I toasted, then took a sip. "Nope."

We all heartily laughed.

Chris said if I didn't like that wine, I wouldn't like any wine.

I gave him my glass. He finished the bottle, which sounds like a lot but it only had three glasses of wine in it. It was the only alcohol he had to drink that weekend. I was a little uncomfortable having two cases of beer in the fridge and two bottles of wine on the kitchen counter, but as Joe says, "A little uncomfortable, we can work with."

And I am… still working on it.

In September, Chris accompanied me to my high school reunion. He ordered a mead called "Zombie Killer." I asked to try it. It smelled decent and it tasted much better than the wine. Still, I stopped at one sip.

Ashley and her husband visited again in October. They brought in their suitcases, an air mattress… and a case of beer. I wasn't expecting that, and I wasn't thrilled, but I didn't say anything. I reminded myself that it hadn't been an issue last time.

Chris had no beer or wine while we were home. He did order one drink when we went out to dinner but didn't finish it. I still get irritated when his friends talk about getting drunk and make it out to be the most important item on their to-do lists. Thankfully, he has only a couple of those friends and it isn't something they do frequently. Regardless, they're good people and I've come to enjoy their company.

My challenges around others' drinking taught me a lot about assumptions and the harm they can do to relationships. For example, if I stuck to my assumptions about how a few drinks might change Chris as a husband, it could have seriously damaged our marriage. It helped when Sandra pointed out that, based on my rebellious choice of style, people might make a few assumptions about me as well.

My love of wearing leather began when my dad and I rode his motorcycle through the country. Unable to bear the pungent smell of the farm animals, I'd touch my nose to my dad's shoulder. The odor of manure would dissipate and my nostrils would instead be filled with the wholesome scent of his leather jacket. The smell comforted me and it still does.

Later, wearing black leather or carrying a purse with spikes and chains also brought me a measure of comfort, albeit in a different way. It gave me the exoskeleton I needed to protect my weak, thin body. It gave me courage.

Whenever I watched '80s movies with my mom, she would point out the bad boys and girls with their heavy metal big hair, boho skirts, studded vests and large pendant necklaces. She said that was her style growing up. I adapted that style, giving it a modern spin and making it my own. I once was offered a fashion retail job during a walk-in interview.

Interviewer: "What are three staples you always have in your closet?"

My response: "Lace, leather, and leopard print." (I secretly geeked at my spontaneous use of alliteration.)

I still enjoy the Renaissance Festival, despite the memories of my husband's pub crawl that once upset me so. I bought a steampunk costume and asked my favorite performer, Manolete the Pyro Gyro, for a picture. It was another memory-worthy birthday. My dad encouraged me to compete in the costume contest. I entered as "Steampunk Stella." Each contestant was asked why they loved the Renaissance Festival. I said it had been a tradition ever since I was a little girl. I loved the costumes and how anyone could be who they wanted; they could be their unique selves and be celebrated for it. I also enjoyed the food and shows. The audience cheered and clapped. I won "Most Historical." Chris said I probably would have won "Crowd Favorite" if any of the other costumes could have passed for historical. A unique costume with new fashionable accessories made me confident enough to speak with a performer and win a costume contest. How cool is that? Plus, I had my family cheering me on. I can do almost anything with their support. Keep this in mind for yourself and your loved ones.

Review and Reflect

What is something you had a sincere disdain for even though reputable sources confirmed it was harmless and/or provided health benefits?

_____

_____

_____

Did this strain your relationships and impact your daily happiness?

Yes   No

Did you eventually budge on this belief or soften your opinion of it?

Yes   No

If not, what can you do to lessen your reaction?

_____

_____

_____

10

Setbacks Happen

No matter how well we plan, no matter how committed we are to our self-care, there will be circumstances beyond our control that can throw us off our game. The key is not to judge ourselves and to get back on track as soon as possible.

For several months I had been doing well in all areas of my life, then things started going downhill again. Distractions, schedule conflicts, and inevitable, unexpected changes led me to a familiar path, one I didn't care to take again. I was starting to spiral into anger, depression and paranoia, so I took eight workdays off to get my life in order. I spent most of my Family Medical Leave Act time speaking with an attorney about a ridiculous lawsuit. I won't discuss its nature, but know that it pushed me to my breaking point.

It was a particularly busy time at my job, and I had an accelerated workload that required me to work ten-hour days. I stopped going to the gym. My protein shakes and Gatorade were replaced with a family-size package of chocolate chip cookies and sugary coffee. Before that week, I never drank coffee. By my second week of overtime, my body was demanding it. Plus, I ate two Dairy Queen Blizzards in the same week. I felt guilty and judged.

By the sixth two-coffee day, my anxiety had taken on a life of its own. My bouncy legs hit and shook the desk. My loud, immature hand farts distracted my colleagues. My eye twitch annoyed me. My pent-up energy had me taking one-minute walks around the department. A friend had suggested the walks. It was supposed to help me stay still long enough to focus on the task at hand. Then, as soon as the caffeine drained from my bloodstream and my eyelids began to close, my brain would gripe, "Coffee!"

"No!" I vehemently replied. "You're not getting a second cup today. You're not having coffee ever again!"

The little twerp fought back with a caffeine withdrawal headache. It lasted for two and a half days. I flooded my body with water, Gatorade, and the occasional orange juice. I stood my ground. Coffee was not going to help me be more productive. Coffee wasn't going to calm my nerves. I wasn't going to allow it to put me back on FMLA.

As I mentioned earlier, I broke routine. I learned from it. It's great overcoming barriers to self-care and to being your best self.

Once, after Chris and I moved into our current home, I went downstairs to bring him lunch. A bottle of coffee liqueur was sitting on his table. I looked at it in disbelief.

"Coffee liqueur, great," I said, clearly unamused.

I quietly went back upstairs, my mind jumping to all sorts of conclusions. *Our friend brought it over. Chris had bought it when he was out of state and had been hiding it from me all this time.* Chris came upstairs and we talked about it, though I didn't have to say a word. My anger and concern made my face unrecognizable. Chris told me he had ordered it when he was in California and it had just been delivered that day. I listened, but I was still a little upset. At that time I had made some progress with regard to my attitude about alcohol; we'd even had wine and beer in our home twice. But to me the coffee liqueur was different; I didn't understand why he had ordered it, nor did I think it was okay for him to drink it. I looked up at him and pleaded.

"How long do you think it will last?"

"A few months."

That still seemed too quick for me. I was still struggling. Chris told me he had about an ounce per serving. He nursed it. I didn't have to worry. I hugged him and told him I was sorry for overreacting. I hadn't been prepared to see liqueur, and it threw me. Hence the strong negative reaction.

"I can prepare for your game nights, bar nights, and conventions," I told him, "where drinking is a possibility."

"I know."

"I can't pr-prepare for something that I d-don't know is in our home."

I'm happy to report that it's going much better now. Six months later and that bottle still isn't empty. There's also a nearly full bottle of mead. That bottle is much larger. Again, he pours a small amount, doesn't have it frequently and sips on it. I'm learning to trust my husband. I'm learning to let go of the hate that consumed me. There wasn't a need for it. I'm still concerned about the circumstances that could happen, but I know they're unlikely.

Improvement came gradually. In fact, I'll admit that for the first few days I eyed the bottle to see how much was left. I would glance at it when I went downstairs to do laundry, went over to give Chris a hug, or while we played pool. Each time, I saw that the liquid remained at the same level. Eventually, and with the help of Ashley, I got to break this distrustful habit. Now the bottle is about a quarter from empty, and I only know that because it's on our kitchen counter next to the sink. Moving the bottle upstairs was the best thing Chris could have done. I got used to seeing it. I wasn't surprised any longer. I couldn't fall back into denial that he didn't drink, because it was there every day for me to see.

As I said, there were setbacks, though over time they became less severe. I remember a conversation with my mother-in-law around Christmas, and the raw emotions I'd felt when I first saw the bottle came rushing back.

That same weekend, the guys came over with a twelve-pack and a six-pack. Ashley's husband made a point of letting me know he wasn't going to drink the whole twelve-pack. Well, I certainly hoped not, considering he was only staying until the next morning. He said he saw I was trying and didn't want to push my limits. That meant a lot to me, and I let him know it. In the morning, I felt I had been lied to. The twelve-pack box was in the garbage and the six-pack was gone as well. Chris said he didn't drink cheap beer. A friend said he didn't drink because he was on medication. Listening to them, I felt the return of mistrust and suspicion. Who was lying to me? Did my husband secretly like cheap beer? Did my friend on medications decide to throw caution to the wind? Or did Ashley's husband who said he wouldn't drink the whole twelve-pack down it within the space of a few hours? Did the friend who brought the six-pack down that?

I replayed everything over and over in my head. At that time, I was still obsessing over details, thinking it helped me cope. Instead, it made me a control freak and made matters worse. I felt guilty, because like the bullying mentioned earlier, I knew others had been in worse situations.

My mentor, Shanda, told me it doesn't matter if someone else has been through worse. What matters is how it impacted me and how I came out on the other side.

It came to a head as I drove to my mother's house to celebrate my brother's birthday. One moment I was excited and thinking about family, motivational speaking, and book signings. In the next, my mind chose a tree for me to drive my car into. There was no barrier to stop me. I didn't think about it. There wasn't a voice telling me to do so. I *saw* myself doing it. Tears had been falling and drying for a few miles. I saw a sign for a rest area. I continued to drive. I stared down the trees on both sides of the expressway. I am stronger. When I felt unsafe, I stopped at the rest area. I called my mom, but couldn't speak right away. It was a mix of crying, stuttering, and panicked breaths.

"Mom, I'm okay. I'm pa-ar-rked at a re-re-rest-stop."

"Elicia. Breathe. Just breathe."

"I'm sorry. I-I've been do-doing we-ell."

I started hyperventilating in earnest.

"Esha, honey. Breathe."

I did my best to take some deep breaths and breathe steadily afterward.

"I love my life, but I just thought about driving into a tree and I don't know why!"

"If you did that, I'd have to do the same."

"I don't want that. I'm feeling better. Thank you."

Suddenly, I felt like I was at my first counseling appointment with Joe again. I was asking myself, why now? I had just gotten published twice, celebrated ten years with Chris and five years with my employer. I had seen friends who I worried were becoming distant. I remembered what Joe told me about experiencing these feelings when life is going well. The mind had time to process what I may have suppressed.

"I'll tell everyone you got weepy but spare the details."

"Thank you, Mom. I love you."

"I love you more. Drive safely."

My mom calmed me and I made it to her place safely.

Muting Myths About Suicidal Thoughts

There is a presumption that people who have suicidal thoughts genuinely want to end their life, but this is not always the case. I am not saying this to spark controversy, but simply to shed new light. If you too have experienced this, you know what I'm talking about. You might have fallen apart when a loved one passed or felt alone. You might have felt hammered after taking emotional hit after hit. Thoughts of self-harm might have come to you at those times. It didn't necessarily mean you wanted to die. You just wanted out of that grief. You wanted the loneliness to end. Whatever the case, it is terrifying.

You may worry that your cries for help are interpreted as attention-seeking or weakness. If you feel that you need to speak with someone, please dial the National Suicide Prevention hotline or a local crisis hotline. It is their responsibility to take your concerns seriously and "talk you down from the ledge."

Thoughts of my family and future plans make me evaluate what I'm thinking. If I do this, I won't see them. It will hurt them. I'll miss the next milestone in their life. Also, I think about my goals and what matters most to me. I'm important too. Stay alive for your family, but keep your dreams alive as well. If you're a parent, even a parent to a pet, you are their world. Be there for your baby or your four-legged or winged family member, but don't forget to be there for yourself.

"Believe in yourself and all that you are. Know that there is something inside you that is greater than any obstacle." ~ Christian D. Larson[24]

---

[24] Top 25 Quotes By Christian D. Larson (of 54): A-z Quotes. Retrieved from https://www.azquotes.com/author/18906-Christian_D_Larson

Review and Reflect

How did you overcome a recent setback?

_____

_____

_____

_____

_____

_____

_____

_____

_____

_____

_____

_____

_____

_____

_____

_____

_____

_____

_____

_____

What actions are you taking to avoid this same outcome?

_____

_____

_____

_____

_____

_____

_____

_____

_____

_____

_____

_____

_____

_____

_____

_____

_____

_____

_____

11

Making Strides

Now that I work from home and am on an earlier shift, I can make it to bar nights and other gatherings. I socialize more. My husband invites me to dinner with his friends and coworkers. I enjoy talking with them and eating good food.

Chris has become more considerate of this too. He'll invite me if the food and non-alcoholic beverage selection is decent.

"If a bar doesn't have decent food, and you can only order water, they have no products that interest you."

"Yes. You get it. I'm happy to be included, but if I go out, I want to eat and have a flavored tea, mocktail, or *something*."

"That makes sense."

Working from home has been my game-changer. I no longer cry in the restroom, hyperventilate at my desk, or need to excuse myself from meetings. I'm more productive and efficient. I complete my work on time and help my teammates. Before, I used to take deep breaths, analyze the agenda and anticipate what might happen in team meetings. Now I'm more confident and have no problem speaking up.

Working from home also allows me to easily integrate self-care into my day. I can complete chores on breaks and lunches. When I'm active in my gym routine, I can go to 9Round and come home and shower before I clock in for the day. On the rare occasions I'm late, it's due to a weekend update or slow loading of my virtual desktop, not because I was frantically rushing around to get ready.

During the sunny months, this work arrangement encourages me to be outdoors more. I'll take my lunch outside and soak up some vitamin D. I'll sit on my yard swing and take in nature's paintings and songs. I don't have to think about what I'll wear and there are no concerns about whether I'll make it safely to or from work. I concentrate better on tasks, and since there's only cat traffic in my house, once I'm off the clock, I'm on *my* time. Perhaps the biggest relief, there are no worries about getting trapped in another flood. The dread of driving to and from Detroit used to send my anxiety off the charts. Now that I've been working from home for a year and a half, I actually find myself appreciating the days I do have to go into the office. In addition to talk therapy, learning coping skills, and being compliant on my medication, working from home has been instrumental in lowering my anxiety.

If you have the option to try working from home, I encourage you to do so. If you find you miss socializing or don't have the self-discipline, you can return to your previous work environment. If you do work in an office or somewhere public and experience anxiety, you can try this grounding exercise. It's one of the first tricks Joe taught me. He calls it, "Naming Objects." When you're in a difficult situation and can't leave, look at your surroundings and name what you see. Let's say, for example, that you're a cashier. You see a counter, a cash register, a keyboard, a service bell, customers, sale signs, etcetera. This makes you aware of your surroundings and lessens any dizziness or confusion you may experience. Maybe you're in a cubicle and have less objects to name. After you name what you see, you can describe each one; for example, "wooden desk," "pink Post-it note," "blue writing," and so on. I hope this helps you next time you get overwhelmed at work or in any other situation you feel stuck.

A couple years ago, a thoughtful gentleman brought a red rose for each woman on the team. It was kind, beautiful and unexpected. I kept the rose on my desk for my entire shift. Unfortunately I had nothing to place it in, so it was without water. At the end of the day, the head of the rose was drooping, but still soft. I carried the rose by the stem and lightly cradled its head with my hand. On my commute home, I laid the flower on the dashboard of my car. I drove with extreme care and this prevented the flower from sliding. I was glad that the petals and leaves were undisturbed.

When I arrived home, I told my mom about the kind gift. She suggested I look up methods to help the rose stand again. I found a helpful video that explained how to use hot water, granulated sugar, Aspirin and a misting bottle. I didn't have Aspirin or sugar.

I diagonally cut the stem and placed it into the hot water. Instead of using a misting bottle, I wet my fingers with warm water and lightly rubbed it onto the leaves and petals. The next morning, I was thrilled to find the rose fully open. Each day, I repeated this routine. Each day, I made sure the rose took in sunlight. When the sun started to set, I moved the vase to the kitchen window.

I took pride in learning something new and being able to keep the delicate rose alive. It was an ongoing process I enjoyed. One night I found Nala sitting on the dining room table and, before I could scold her, I saw that the stem was broken. The rose head was dangling and barely attached. I was disappointed but grateful that the red rose still appeared healthy.

At my mom's suggestion, I cut what remained of the stem, then filled a shallow dish with warm water and placed it inside. I made sure the petals received their fair share too. I'm happy to say the rose stayed hydrated and in full bloom.

I ran into a few different obstacles in caring for this rose.

Although I didn't have all the suggested ingredients to save it, I still made the effort. It was worth it. You've probably navigated unexpected obstacles in your life. Most likely, you used the tools available to you and hoped for the best outcome. If you find yourself feeling lost or hopeless, please remember you're worth every effort. Like the rose, you can survive.

Coping with a Grieving Heart

When the lawsuit ended, removing the files related to it eased my mind and helped me to let the trauma go. I used the opposite technique to comfort me after the passing of my maternal grandmother, Grandma P, in October of 2019. I found that surrounding myself with reminders of her brings me comfort. I also keep a picture of my late great-grandma and a small owl memento from my late Grandpa P on my desk. These items help keep my loved ones alive in my heart.

I like to think Grandma P helped me write this part of the book. The second to last time I visited her, she said to do things while I'm young and healthy. This made me want to finish all my projects and cross off everything on my to-do-list. Now, instead of thinking about her passing and her last few days, I think about her life. I feel her love.

My dad, brother, and I used to visit the graves of my cousin and great grandma. I'm not sure if it was too hard emotionally or we simply became too busy, but somewhere along the line those visits stopped. I would like to start visiting my grandma and grandpa's graves, perhaps on holidays and birthdays like my family by marriage does. I think my grandparents would appreciate it. I think it would help us as well.

Coping with mental illness is learning to regulate your emotions so you stay in control, both during normal times and in stressful situations. Coping during mourning is different. You have a valid reason to emotionally react. You aren't trying to let something go or understand your symptoms; you're feeling a loss and learning to live without that person by your side. You're remembering routines, smells, favorite foods, and their laughter. Allow yourself to go back to any memory with your deceased loved one. Look at it fondly and return with a new appreciation. I've done this a lot recently. Yes, every time brought tears, but those tears were a healthy release. They were, dare I say, even spiritual.

In Grandma P's case, I utilized a coping skill even before she passed. Dreading her decline and eventual absence, I wrote a tribute to her, capturing all her amazing qualities and the reasons I loved her. It was therapeutic. I read the tribute to her on our last visit together. She was mostly unresponsive by then, but I hope she heard every word. At her funeral service, the priest beautifully painted Grandma P's life. He said it revolved around God, love, and family. I'd argue it was family, love, and God, but essentially he nailed it.

If you're grieving, I hope you reach out to the people who knew that person best. Your communication can be emotional support to them. It can bring you closer to your loved one. Think of it this way: how can you bend, rather than break?

When Grandma passed, my mom needed me. It was my turn to be strong for her and I was, up until the last thirty minutes of the visitation. I didn't want to leave my grandma's casket. The next day was the service and burial. My big brother pulled me toward him and allowed me to cry snot and tears on the shoulder of his dress shirt and tie. He teared up a bit too. Then my cousin joined us, and it was a group hug at the casket. My brother asked Mom if I was driving home.

"No. She's riding with Mark and me."

"Good. She's in no condition to drive."

A few minutes later, I walked out with my mom and her other half. My brother walked out, burying his face into his wife's shoulder. I felt awful. I had never seen him so distraught. One day, when my mind was quiet, that image played in my head. I felt just the same as before.

On our first Christmas without her, Mom and I paid tribute to Grandma P by recreating her peanut butter fudge and "puke salad." This oddly-named dish is served as a sweet side. Its ingredients are cottage cheese, jello, cool whip, and crushed pineapple. My mom made the fudge and I made the salad, and the consensus was that both were pretty close to Grandma's.

Once or twice a month I would call Grandma at my aunt and uncle's house, where she was living. After she passed I started calling to talk to them. The first time was difficult, but nice. My uncle told me while cleaning out Grandma's writing desk he had found seven packages of pictures. She was proud of all of us.

My uncle and I both took comfort from that call. As much as I was hurting, I felt it had to have been harder on him. Everything was in his name, so the responsibility of handling her belongings and last wishes fell to him.

I encourage you to bend, but not break. Reach out and be there for one another. As my dad told me, "It's okay to be derailed for a little while as long as you find your way back to the track."

Once again, a rose played a small but significant role in my healing. Before we left the mausoleum that day, the funeral coordinator carefully removed flowers from the casket arrangement. Many family members, including myself, took one home. I chose a rose. I placed it in water until it started to wilt two weeks later. Until then, I had been unsure if I wanted to keep the rose in water, hang it to dry, press it in a book, or crumble it into potpourri. In the end I decided to place it in the arms of the angel Grandma P had given me. That angel, along with a bag of groceries and a candy dish, was the last thing she gave me before she passed. I keep positive phrases in the candy dish. Now, I see the angel with her rose every day and think of my grandmother's love and generosity.

Review and Reflect

How do you grieve and honor your loved ones who have passed away?

_____

_____

_____

_____

_____

_____

_____

_____

_____

_____

_____

_____

_____

_____

Getting Back on Track

After going several months without exercising, I finally made it a priority again. I was told the muscle memory would be there and it would be easier to build muscle this time. I knew it would be like the first day when I took multiple breaks and could barely catch my breath. That was okay. I went and I was welcomed by the trainer.

"Tiny Terror! Welcome back! How are you?"

I knew I'd made the right decision.

I did my stretches and visited the water fountain. I remembered the cross, hook and undercut, but needed a refresher for the jab. He showed me again.

As we got to the first station with weights, he told me, "No weights today. Let's ease into it."

That worked. The round kicks still felt natural, but my balance was off. I was happy to see I still had great form for my squats. Both trainers, who had worked with me quite a bit before I took my unexpected hiatus, complimented me on that. The trick is to act like you're about to sit on a chair. Keep your knees above or behind your toes. Your back should be relatively straight. Don't look down. Look straight ahead.

I did every round and took multiple breaks, as expected. I was proud to do it. I felt great afterward. The next time I went in, we got into some light weights, which I held while doing the burnout exercises. These usually require more stamina and are done for the final minute of each round.

The time after that, my core work was still pitiful, though thankfully my balance was improving. I sat on the floor with my hands by my rear and my legs in the air. I moved my legs from left to right and over a standing object. I knocked it over the first time and I missed it the rest. More improvement. Going to the kickboxing gym is still fun for me. I saw a couple of people from my morning crew and was moved when one sweet woman hugged me. I also started walking and jogging around the block with Chris, and though I slowed him down a bit we had a nice time together. Again, my endurance is still low. I breathed heavily after each jog. He checked on me.

I'd gained a little weight, which also might have contributed to the difficulty. I had always been thin and didn't need to work to maintain my figure. Now, I'm still thin but have a small roll just above my waistline; my clothes don't fit as well. As motivation for myself (and a shock to family and friends), I asked Chris to take pictures of me in my workout gear with my "bulging" belly and a hint of a double chin.

Chris had to help me zip up my sports bra. I was busting out of it. This is the most I've ever had up top and I found I wasn't looking forward to losing it. Chris agreed.

"I can tell going back to the gym isn't going to be good for your boobs," he said.

We both laughed. I love his humor.

I posted that picture, along with one before my break from working out. My abs were definitely more defined in the older one. I said it was my "before and after" in reverse. I like being real with people. It helps keep me accountable. I want to be healthy mentally and physically. Hopefully, I'll see the results of that desire - and my gym appointments – in the next photo.

Review and Reflect

What progress have you made so far? Where did you start? How do you feel about your accomplishments? What was the best thing you did that helped you feel better and like yourself?

_____

_____

_____

_____

_____

_____

_____

_____

_____

_____

_____

_____

_____

_____

_____

_____

_____

_____

_____

12

Understanding Dreams
and Reducing Unconscious Anxiety

As I wrote this next section I was aware that it may not be relatable to everyone. That said, I have had numerous issues sleeping (i.e. being afraid to sleep and trouble staying asleep) and felt it was crucial to include it. Like other barriers, I saw a problem, reached out for guidance, and tried to fix it. I gave this challenging experience meaning. Two of my cousins helped me. To protect their identities, I refer to them as Cousin Raven and Cousin Wolf.

Dream Diary: Witchcraft, Self Defense, and Humility

On the Insight Timer application, I listened to Step 1: Reawaken Your Confidence, Night Version. It must have done something, because I had a strange dream that I fought a witch and won. I went to a diner afterward. My hair was sweaty and in a ponytail. Someone gave me a hat. Five male waiters were fighting to wait on me. They were dancing, tossing menus and doing magic tricks. In my dream, I joked as Chris came in and sat down with me.

"Wow! Sweaty hair in a ponytail must be a good look for me."

During our time at the diner, a trivia question was asked.

"What holiday is celebrated with sugar skulls, costumes and grave primping?"

I called out, "Día de los Muertos."

My answer was correct. As we were leaving the diner, we saw the witch again; this time she was accompanied by her coven. I gave them a stern look and nod. They left us alone. We returned home. I took off my hat and a hand-sized clump of hair came out with it. Maybe, it was reminding me to be modest or humble. It was interesting, indeed.

Dream Interpretations by Cousin Raven

One of my cousins has been interpreting her dreams for years. Occasionally, I speak with her about mine. She said the restaurant reminded her of Psalm 23. Since I'm not familiar with scripture I looked it up and immediately saw what she meant.

"Even though I walk through the valley of the shadow of death, I will fear no evil, for You are with me; Your rod and Your staff, they comfort me. You prepare a table for me in the presence of my enemies; You anoint my head with oil; my cup overflows." [25]

Cousin Raven believed the five waiters represented angels at my service. She also informed me that witchcraft includes three key elements – manipulation, intimidation and domination – and suggested that I might have been fighting those elements in my waking life. On the other hand, witchcraft can also signify an inner transformation. Dreaming of hats, according to information she sent from dreammoods.com, relates to hiding an aspect of oneself.

These interpretations deeply resonated with me. According to my psychiatrist, I have all forms of anxiety. I used to hide, yet I tried

---

[25] Psalm 23:4; New American Standard Bible

to be open with people. Prioritizing self-care, establishing care with a psychiatrist and getting approved for FMLA had been like my inner transformation. Then again, I had felt a lot of intimidation around my artwork, my work, thoughts of furthering my education and having to possibly go to court to deal with the lawsuit.

Cousin Raven said the reference to Día de los Muertos was symbolic as well. I loved Spanish class and the culture I'd learned about in high school. She said it may have meant I was focusing too much on my past. She was right. I often reflected on my past, though it was to appreciate my progress.

Dream Diary: Instantly Deaf

In another dream, I cautiously drove by car accidents on my way to work, like I did in my waking life before I started working from home. Once I entered the office, a friend and I were walking to a meeting when suddenly a blaring siren went off. It startled me and I fell down, covering my ears in the hallway. I started to tell my friend what happened. She looked at me with worry in her eyes and said there was no alarm. No one else heard it. Then, I couldn't hear at all. I was deaf.

Dream Interpretations by Cousin Raven

Cars represent how people navigate through life or circumstances, endeavors or even their own persona and emotions. Cousin Raven said being on my way to work probably meant I was working on myself and my own issues. The sound symbolized my struggles. That's why no one else could hear it. The issues were so great they resulted in my impairment.

In her experience, unresolved issues become the filter that everything passes through. The deafness could have meant if the issues were not dealt with I might not have heard or understood things that were important. Possibly, I would have blocked out the rest of the world as a coping mechanism. She was right again. I had previously tried to block out Chris's drinking and pretended that he would stop. That led to me being cruel and not understanding how I was harming him.

First Phone Reading: Dream Analysis

Joe helped me work on my unresolved issues and the bad dreams became infrequent, only to come back with a vengeance later on. Since my family doctor, counselor, and psychiatrist couldn't help me, I went a different route, one that was definitely outside my comfort zone and belief system.

I contacted a local psychic who specialized in dream analysis and scheduled a phone appointment. She was pleasant to speak with and had a lovely voice. When she asked if I had recurring dreams, I said no but I did have recurring *themes*. She then shared some enlightening insight.

The most significant thing she said to me was, "Your brain is like a machine. It's methodical. It's meant to solve problems. When you go to sleep, your brain is trying to solve an old problem. It thinks you need to escape a dangerous situation that you're no longer in."

This too resonated with me. My brain was accustomed to being in a depressed and anxious state. That explained why I was always trying to get away from someone or something in my dreams. My brain hadn't caught up with my progress and my recovery.

Where I saw fear and disgust in the decaying animals in my dreams, she saw personal growth and hope. I told her I once saw a rotting pig standing on two legs standing by a dumpster. The skin and meat were falling off it. The psychic was excited by this. She said the peeling of the skin and the meat next to a dumpster was like my psyche, purging what was holding me back and throwing it away!

She said if I could take the emotion out of my dreams and approach them with "intellectual curiosity," I would find meaningful symbolism.

In the meantime, I also spoke with Cousin Wolf, who reads tarot cards and practices Reiki, and she was only too happy to help. Cousin Wolf was on the same track as the psychic and Cousin Raven. She said that my dreams aren't nightmares, but messages from guides. She agreed with the psychic reader's strategy.

The psychic also told me pigs are loyal and will seek out specific pigs to hang out with. She said the image of the pig by the dumpster on two legs could also be alluding to a toxic friendship. I thought about the friendship I'd told Joe about in my first appointment. It wasn't toxic. It was *missing*. My friend hadn't spoken with me in years.

This same old friend was in a different dream the psychic analyzed for me. I apologize in advance if these are too graphic. This is why I don't watch horror movies – I have enough playing in my mind while I sleep.

In this dream, my friend and I were in a plantation house in the 1840s. All the walls were painted crimson. A cook was trying to serve us a person she had boiled. When my friend and I refused, the cook threatened to boil and eat us too. We ran. The house continued to get larger as we ran. We didn't make it out. I woke up when she caught us.

I also recounted being rescued by others in my dreams. The psychic pointed out that I was doing all the work and giving others in my dream the credit. That tied into real life too.

She asked how long I'd been having nightmares, to which I replied, "Twenty-one years." She said there was a teeny tiny chance that an entity from my dad's house had attached itself to me. She doubted it, but just in case she gave me some simple banishing and cord-cutting rituals. (This was the part that was outside my comfort zone.)

We ended the call talking about lucid dreaming and dream programming. That night, I tried to program my dream to be about my trip with Chris to Mackinac Island. That is where he proposed to me. It was unbelievably romantic. I closed my eyes and visualized the scenery. I tried to smell the homemade chocolate fudge, hear the bicycles passing by, and feel the breeze coming off the Great Lakes. My mind wandered to work, a few scary images, and driving. Like meditation, I brought my focus back to Mackinac Island.

That night, I dreamt I was at a hockey game. I joked with my husband.

"I tried to program my dream to take me to Mackinac Island. I think it took me a bit north. I was watching a hockey game. I think it took me to Canada."

Chris humored me. "I think you need to work on your aim."

Later I spoke with Cousin Wolf again. She said there was no entity attached to me; she knew because she checked my aura, as well as my brother's, each time she saw us. We are "*sensitives*," she said, and could be susceptible to such occurrences.

In high school, I dreamt about a motorcycle accident. A man in his fifties hit a guardrail and flew off his bike. The man was in critical condition. When I woke, I immediately called my dad. My panic grew as I got this voicemail.

Frantically, I pleaded, "Dad, I just had an awful dream. If you're okay, please call me. P-please be okay. I love you."

Hot tears and pain tore through me as I worried about my dad. I turned on the news and saw the same scene from my dream. It was real. My dad called me while I watched the report. I was grateful to hear his voice. I explained what I saw. I asked him to check on his friends. He said they went riding last night, and thankfully they were all okay.

There have been other situations where I became a nervous wreck out of nowhere, to later find out something terrible happened down the road or nearby. The things the reader and I discussed held a lot of weight. Eventually, I may schedule another reading. She told me she usually uses tarot cards and other objects when performing dream readings, so I think I'll stick with the phone.

After speaking with the psychic, my dreams became less frightening and intense. Each morning, I wrote down a few sentences and tried to decipher the message.

While writing this book, I had dreams of little girls and their dads lining up to enter my childhood home, where my dad still resides. They were at the side door. One of the girls who came in told me she had to leave through the front door. I found the symbolism in this to be my vulnerability of sharing my lowest and private moments in this book. Cousin Wolf said I was absolutely right. She said the girl having to leave through the front door was my psyche saying, "I'll have to accept readers' opinions of my book and of me." I opened myself up to that.

Several times, I woke up in the dark to see a spider coming down onto me. Cousin Wolf explained seeing the spider descending and spinning a web meant I was creating my own space. To her, it meant I was almost done fixing myself. That was great news. Maybe the spiders would leave soon.

When my dreams took me inside dimly lit bathrooms, she

interpreted that to mean that I was confused. Cousin Wolf reminded me that I have worked through my issues and she's been watching from the sidelines. She said what I call nightmares is my anxiety manifesting and taking control of my unconscious. Since I'm in control during the day, it activates at other times. She suggested I try Emotional Freedom Technique (EFT) tapping. From some online author friends, I knew the bare minimum – that it was focusing on getting rid of a negative thought while repeatedly tapping on different pressure points on the body. Cousin Wolf affirmed that the goal was to get rid of my anxiety and said she knew someone she trusted that could help me.

Cousin Wolf also asked if I had a dream catcher.

"Yes, it's above my side of the bed."

"Do you open your curtains or blinds during the day?"

"Yes."

"Does the sunlight hit the dream catcher?"

"No."

"Do me a favor. Tomorrow, open the blinds and set your dream catcher in the window. Yours is full. You need to cleanse it."

I laughed a little. "Yeah. That makes sense. I'll do that."

She explained that it was a Native American legend. I was starting to think spiritually. That could be another step in the right direction. The next day, I did as she suggested. I took a picture and sent it to Cousin Wolf.

I had a follow-up appointment with my psychiatrist the same day. I told her that my cousin suggested EFT tapping. She hadn't heard of it so I explained the concept while she looked it up.

"I think it might be mind over matter," I said, "but I respect and love my cousin. I think I might want to talk with her friend."

My psychiatrist warned me that it might reopen old wounds that I was over. She said I'd come a long way and didn't think I needed it, but she left the decision to me.

One weekend, I was home alone. Friday and Saturday were great. One of my friends came over, then I went to Sandra's housewarming party and had a nice time there too. I came home and got ready for bed. Everything was normal until I was awoken by a male voice. I lay as still as could be, my breathing ragged, my heart pounding out of my chest. The worst part was that I was wearing a sleep mask and couldn't make myself remove it. I couldn't tell whether someone was really there or not. I also couldn't see the clock, but it felt like I was laying there in horror for at least an hour. The whole time I kept repeating in my head, *It's not real. No one's here.* Eventually, I exhausted myself and slept. That was the last night I wore a sleep mask to bed.

The next night I was so scared that I drove to Jessica's house two blocks away. When I got there, I felt ashamed and embarrassed. She gave me one of her best hugs and told me it was okay. I slept in our other friend's room. She was away for the weekend. I took my rescue pill and fell asleep.

The next time Chris left for a weekend, I prepared myself. There's a show Chris and I watch that is great but can sometimes be creepy. I told him how I was feeling on edge and asked that we stop watching it just for the week. He understood. I also told my mom that he was going out of town and I would be alone.

"You're welcome to stay here."

"Thanks Mom, but Jessica and I have our appointments Saturday. We're going to lunch afterward. I need to do this. I feel that if I can get through this weekend okay, whatever fear is trying to come back will go away."

"Okay. I'm here if you need me."

"Thanks, Mom. Love you."

"I love you more. You'll be fine."

The first night I was home alone, I changed into pajamas around eight-thirty, then made some hot tea and sipped it while I journaled. I was calm, though a bit teary-eyed at first, but by the time I finished my tea and wrote four pages I felt okay. By nine-forty p.m. I had brushed my teeth, put my body pillow in the bed, taken a Xanax, turned on a rain app and slipped into bed. I know. It's early. My grandparents stay up later than I do. A consistent early bedtime benefits me and I'm not ashamed of it. As I laid there, I remembered a prayer the psychic had shared with me. It couldn't hurt, right? I quietly recited, "To all my ancestors, known and unknown, I request you help me sleep." I thought of my great grandma, my cousins, and my Grandma and Grandpa P. I repeated it again. I asked to not have nightmares or night terrors. "To all my ancestors, known and unknown, I request peaceful sleep." Then I continued to lay there, wide awake, for a minimum of an hour and thirty minutes.

The rain app helped. I heard the furnace start but missed the banging and clanging that it made before that. I turned my media volume higher than usual. While I let the rain fall and cracking thunder drown out the city noise, I completed a peaceful sleep meditation I had memorized. I tried to let the tension in my face, neck, limbs, and body go. I tried to release all worries too. When the slightest bit of a creepy sensation began to take over, I opened my eyes and looked around the room. Each time, I saw nothing and no one. That gave me power. That put me back in control. The next night, I did the same, but I was weepy and did not sleep as well.

My paternal aunt suggested I keep a jasmine plant in my bedroom to help me sleep. I started looking into the science behind it and learned there are several plants that help relieve anxiety and insomnia. Jasmine can relieve anxiety. Lavender lowers heart rate, blood pressure, and stress levels. Valerian was traditionally used to treat insomnia. Extract from the valerian root is used in calming teas. Gardenia relieves stress. It's said to be a "natural tranquilizer, without harmful side-effects." The passionflower can improve mood, relieve anxiety, and pain. It reportedly "helps induce sleep."[26] Essential oils from the chamomile flower "can help people who suffer from nightmares." Vanilla Honey Chamomile tea is a regular wind-down beverage for me. I might need to add this flower to the bedroom too. Chris might soon confuse our room for a greenhouse.

Review and Reflect

How have you gone outside your comfort zone to find a solution?

_____

_____

_____

_____

_____

_____

_____

_____

_____

_____

[26] Lipworth, Elaine. "Thrive Global." Thrive Global (blog), June 25, 2019. https://thriveglobal.com/stories/bringing-nature-intoplants-help-aid-improve-sleep-nature-bedroom-relaxing/?fbclid=IwAR3GJbDxNvp7jqCC60inuQHDme3t3sZyZ_8jDZxBjI4nZ_Quo6BoAVlEPUc.

What do you do when you're unable to fall or stay asleep?

_____

_____

_____

_____

_____

_____

_____

_____

_____

_____

_____

_____

_____

_____

_____

_____

_____

_____

_____

_____

_____

_____

13

Wrapping Up Mental Health

During that stressful lawsuit and my decline at work, there were several physical symptoms of anxiety and depression that I mistook for pregnancy. I went five months without a menstrual cycle. I craved comfort foods and anything else made me nauseous. I slept most of the day after work and several hours on weekends. I took multiple home pregnancy tests and had one completed at the doctor's office. My doctor told me that it's normal for a female's body to react this way when under immense stress.

After Grandma P's funeral, I felt the familiar nausea and fatigue. I cried every night. My psychiatrist advised I take my rescue medication before bed for seven days to help me sleep. I started sleeping through the night but was still drowsy during the day. Again, I wasn't eating much. My stomach was telling me it was sick. Sometimes eating made it better; other times, it worsened the nausea. After the seven days were completed, the stomach pain and pre-vomit feelings faded. It could have been the sudden increase in Xanax that added to my discomfort. I wasn't alone in this and neither are you.

I can't stress this enough. Your mental health is just as important as your physical health, and the two are intimately linked. Anxiety, depression, suicidal ideations, and other symptoms don't discriminate by economic class, race, gender, or age. I remember taking a picture of a white Lamborghini at my counselor's office and sending the picture to my husband with a similar caption.

"A psychiatrist probably owns it," he joked.

I don't know if that was the case or not. It was the only time I saw a Lamborghini in that parking lot in the five years I've gone there. Then again, I wouldn't doubt it.

This book is by no means an exhaustive list of the mental and behavioral health challenges. It simply covers what I live with and can elaborate on. Please be sensitive to others. The best you can do for them and yourself is to learn their reality then try to make things easier for both of you. Remember that symptoms and severity vary from person to person. I saw something online about not comparing plates. One plate might be ceramic and able to hold a lot, while another might be paper that bends or rips when the same amount of food is placed upon it. I thought that analogy was spot-on for mental health.

Some people may have learned how to handle more; others may need sturdier supports. Again, I've been both of these people. Give yourself time to process, heal and grow.

Do you remember cleaning your room as a kid and finding things that used to bring you hours of joy, but hadn't played with in months? Reading my poetry from high school brought me similar feelings of nostalgia.

I realized I'd overused the words: *rare, glow, light, alone, lonely, fear,* and *true.* There was a recurring theme of being my unique self and not wanting to let others down. At age twelve, I wrote about worrying if my writing would ever be good enough. How I wish I would have taken my poetry to a counselor back then. He could have diagnosed me and started treatment much sooner. My early poetry showed signs of depression and anxiety. I also mentioned God, Him, and the Creator a few times, which, as I was never very religious, was both odd and interesting.

I wrote about sweatshops, race cars, and even Anne Frank. I found a few poems that were light-hearted and uplifting. I'm glad I wasn't all doom and gloom.

Still, rereading my poems and looking at the dates and times brought me both tears and smiles. I remembered what I was going through. Another thing that stood out was the times at which I wrote them – several were after nine p.m. and some were written as late as three in the morning. These too were signs, in this case of my sleep issues and possibly night terrors. I vividly remember writing by moonlight and holding a flashlight under the covers to read and write. Each of my poems had small doodles. A few were intentional and went with the context. The rest were random shapes and cross hatches in the margins. This could have indicated an overwhelming amount of thoughts at once and an inability to focus. This affected me as an adult at home and in the office. I'm more self-aware now and can spot these things. Plus, I take a low dose medication for ADHD. It mostly quiets my mind at night and increases my focus during the day.

Today, writing means as much to me as it did back then. I told my mom about my poems. She said maybe I'll be inspired to write poetry again, this time with happier themes. I appreciated her well wishes. I've heard from other authors that pain and turmoil fueled their writing too. I needed to find the passion for beautiful subject matter and inspiring content. My blog was the beginning of that.

As a child, I remember how angry I was when I caught my brother and old friend reading my diary. While writing this book, I sometimes felt similarly raw and exposed, even though I was now voluntarily sharing my most vulnerable and challenging times in hopes that it would make a lasting positive impact. In some ways, I'm still like the little girl who wanted to be liked and understood;

the difference is I've learned that I don't *need* to be liked by everyone. Only I can assign the value of my self-worth, and the same goes for you. It is my dearest hope that reading about my story has helped you better understand me, you, and the conditions discussed. If you have a loved one experiencing anxiety and depression, I hope you have a better understanding of the treacherous path they are navigating and your role in seeing them through.

On New Year's Day, I told my husband that I wasn't too anxious, scared, or depressed to shower regularly in 2019. That had been an issue in the past. I used to be afraid that someone would enter our home and hurt me. I used to worry about my own actions as well. It's strange that these concerns were present only when I showered. Like I mentioned earlier, it's when I'm most vulnerable.

This progress is a result of alternating a number of items and tools. You don't need to buy the products I mentioned. I have no stock in the companies. I've simply tried almost anything to get a handle on my conditions and emotions. My doctor and mental health providers are on board with all my efforts. They are the backbone of my treatment. The only home remedies that I know of and adamantly will not try are medical marijuana, CBD oil, and hallucinogenic mushrooms; I also will not criticize your *regulated* use of the remedies listed above. Instead, I will praise you in taking a step forward.

I encourage you to use what you learned from my personal stories and trials. I challenge you to look for methods outside of what was mentioned. Some things need to be done on your own. For other parts of your recovery, you will find a support system is beneficial. When I tried to isolate myself so as not to bother anyone or embarrass myself, my support system came to me. I'm grateful they showed me they care, that they're there for me, and that I matter. Their messages were well received and needed. I tried to only let in pleasant experiences. I limited time spent watching the news and stopped watching horror movies years ago. I sought out joyful videos, enlightening books, and meaningful conversations.

I shared what I learned about mental health. I started blogging about my struggles and accomplishments. No victory was too small. Soon after, my posts were shared and supporters told me I inspired them. In truth, they motivated me. The more they said I helped them or they were proud of me, the more I wanted to share with them.

My wise cousin once told me you see the good in others that you want to see in yourself. I find that fitting. I see kindness and determination in my friends. I see affection and protection in my parents and grandparents. I witness strength in my loved ones. I took on these traits.

I try to be kind to everyone. I smile, compliment, and check in on people. I'm determined to be the best version of myself, live a better quality of life, and give hope to others. I'm affectionate to my family and friends. I protect my wellness and happiness from intrusive thoughts and unpleasant stimuli. I'm strong for seeking treatment and continuing my existence when my mind fed me numerous ways to end it.

Acknowledging a mental illness and learning to understand it is empowering. You're taking back the power that seemed to flow out of your body when that illness swallowed you. You gain a unique power and strength from your new coping skills. You get a second chance. That's how I think about my life in treatment. It's a second chance for joy, love, respect, peace, and a fulfilling life. You're worthy of that life.

I hope you work through denial, acceptance, self-care, and personal development. Don't be surprised if you repeat some stages or go in a different order. Mental health is both cyclical and unpredictable. Above all, I hope you find a new confidence and self-worth that cannot be diminished by external factors. I wish you all the best this life has to offer.

Review and Reflect

What stage are you in now? How do you know?

_____

_____

_____

_____

_____

_____

_____

_____

_____

_____

_____

_____

_____

_____

_____

How will you know when you've progressed to the next?

_____

_____

_____

_____

_____

_____

_____

_____

_____

_____

_____

_____

_____

What behaviors of yours do you recognize being a manifestation of your conditions?

_____

_____

_____

_____

_____

_____

_____

_____

_____

_____

_____

_____

_____

How can you control those behaviors?

_____

_____

_____

_____

_____

_____

_____

_____

_____

_____

_____

_____

14

Empowering Others Through Social Media

In this chapter you'll see how my insecurities were planted years ago, and how I came to recognize them and adjusted my outlook and behavior. In my small community, I started to become an enthusiast for self-care and mental health. The growing support reassured me I was fulfilling my purpose. I no longer felt like a "personal cone." Take that, gym class bully!

Several people thanked me for being a ray of sunshine. My self-esteem flourished when I opened up to others about my barriers and setbacks. It helped me come to terms with the situation at hand.

There are many people like you. They are working through similar obstacles. You don't have to be alone anymore.

I belong to two mental health support groups on Facebook. Thanks to my fantastic support system, I realize I don't need it as much. Instead, I find myself offering support to the group members. If you're going to join these groups, set an exposure limit. This isn't a setting in the group. This is something you regulate on your own. These groups have hundreds to thousands of members, many of them who share some pretty devastating things. I find that if I read those posts for too long or too frequently it affects my mood and thoughts. Also, read the rules. The groups may require a disclaimer for posts that may trigger group members. There's the auditor in me again.

I started sharing information about medical tests, taking medications for the first time, and establishing a self-care routine. I received positive responses. I'm surprised how many distant friends told me they had panic attacks at work or isolated themselves, because they didn't want people to see their symptoms.

Now, I see my friends healing. Their posts are about letting go of what hurt them and learning to love themselves. I am all for that. I am happy for them.

Blogging with a Purpose

I never understood why parents told their children, "Big kids don't cry." Yes, they do. Adults cry too. It's feeling emotions and having a physical response. It's what allows us to be sympathetic for others' losses and pain. It's what helps us be empathetic about a difficult situation. When crying overpowers the conversation and lasts long after it's over, that's when something else might be responsible.

It's funny how people tell me I inspire them. They, in turn, inspire me. When I had a bad day, I used to worry that I was going to let others down. Now, I realize it's more important to show them that having a bad day is normal and recovering from it is greater. I appreciate the support I receive. Friends have let me know simply asking about their day or posting about a struggle or accomplishment has helped them immeasurably. One work friend thanked me for being compassionate and said I could sprinkle her with "dazzle dust" anytime. I thought that was sweet, like her.

Another friend saw my posts and decided she was going to get organized, go to her appointments and start going to the gym, and she did! I love that accountability. When we work to be our best selves and to show hope for others, life has more meaning and, amazingly, becomes easier. I don't worry about looking weak or broken. I think about how others might need to hear about my lazy day in pajamas, no shower and almost forgetting to eat. Then they need to hear about me making up the next day by doing house-work, going to the gym, and blogging. It doesn't take much to make a difference.

Another friend just started blogging and I offered her insight and encouraged her to write freely. I'm proud that she has begun this healing process.

Social media is not a stressor for me. I hide political posts and unfollow friends who constantly post about drama. I follow authors, bloggers, animal pages, happiness pages, and my family. My newsfeed makes me glow from happiness and love. I see my nephew's first walk, my mom's new painting, and my dad's trip to Switzerland. I love it. Everyone is doing something that matters. That's what I allow in my life.

When I post about a difficult day, week or month, the same people are there to help me and remind me that I've been there for them. It's a good feeling.

You inspire me. You inspire me to make it a good day and a day worth sharing on social media. I see a movement of empowerment. We're giving each other the tools to do something on our own. We're giving each other strength and confidence. That's what I want to do. That's why I blog. That's why I wrote this book. If you would like to keep up with me on social media, please visit my website, www.eliciaraprager.com and follow my author profiles:

Facebook: facebook.com/Elicia-Raprager-Author-398108577675608
Instagram: @EliciaRaprager or www.instagram.com/eliciaraprager
Pinterest: www.pinterest.com/EliciaRapragerAuthor
Amazon Author Central: amazon.com/author/elicia_raprager

Because of social media, I have met unique, talented, caring people. I am beyond grateful. If it wasn't for losing control of my emotions and life, I wouldn't have written this book to reach out and help relate to all of you. It's okay to get help. It's okay, no matter your age, race, gender or socioeconomic status. Please don't let stigmas and stereotypes stop you from living the life you and your loved ones deserve. I hope I will get a chance to hear about your progress and success. You are an amazing individual. Don't let depression and anxiety hide that from you.

I was empowered by Gretchen Rubin's book, *The Happiness Project*. She focused on improving a different aspect of her life each month for one year. Her goal was to become happier and she shared her efforts on her blog. I was amazed by her and enthralled by her book.[27] Jessica recommended I read it. Now I'm making the same recommendation to you.

Another online friend was going through a separation. She told me she was reading my blogs and writing down notes. She said it helped. That means a lot to me. Something like a separation or divorce changes your way of living. It's like starting over. I'm honored that my words could lend her some support during that transitional time of her life.

There have been a couple of online friends I didn't talk with much but knew they were given more to handle than any one person should. For two weeks, I made those two friends my priority. I sent cute memes and checked in. It meant a lot to them. It took little effort and no energy, but gave them much-needed support. That's my mission in life.

As I've said to friends, if it wasn't for going undiagnosed and becoming unmanageable, I wouldn't have the same appreciation

---

[27] Rubin, Gretchen. **The** *Happiness Project: Or, Why I Spent a Year Trying to Sing in the Morning, Clean My Closets, Fight Right, Read Aristotle, and Generally Have More Fun.* Harper Collins, 2018.

for life and my progress. I wouldn't be able to relate to others with similar struggles. I wouldn't be able to share my story and help you. This is my sparkly silver lining in the dark stormy sky.

Share a smile. Stay inspired.

Review and Reflect

What inspires you?

_____

_____

_____

_____

_____

_____

_____

_____

What empowers you?

_____

_____

_____

_____

_____

_____

_____

_____

How do you currently use social media platforms?

_____

_____

_____

_____

_____

_____

_____

_____

What actions will you take to make social media a more positive experience?

_____

_____

_____

_____

_____

_____

_____

_____

Stay Inspired and Keep Smiling!

Thank you for reading my book. I would appreciate it if you leave an honest review on Amazon and post about it on social media, using the hashtag, #ReadShareaSmile. This will help get my story noticed by people who need it most.

Take Care of Yourself and Your Loved Ones

Spread mental health awareness
Know the signs
Know your resources
Know you matter

I believe in you.

Elicia Raprager

ABOUT THE AUTHOR

Elicia Raprager is a contributing author to two bestselling books, *The Grateful Soul: The Art and Practice of Gratitude* and to *Inspirations: 101 Uplifting Stories for Daily Happiness.* Her romantic short story, "The Huron Suite," was featured in the July/August issue of the RAC Magazine. As a child, Elicia wrote and drew; in her teen years, both became passions. When her mental health declined, she returned to these hobbies. Although Elicia struggled, she challenged herself to remain positive. The best compliment Elicia can hear is, "You inspired me." Today, Elicia opens up about her mental health on her blog and social media, and has been overwhelmed by encouragement and gratitude. She prioritizes self-care for mental and physical health. *Share a Smile: Thriving in Life and Treatment* is Elicia's first solo book. To learn more about her work, go to www.eliciaraprager.com and visit her Amazon Author Page.